About the Author

an Be Tter world has been endowed with an abundance of energy, which he has focused in many directions throughout his life. His career to date has been wholly people-orientated from which he has drawn his diverse experiences in writing this book. Born in Holloway, North London N19 and bred in Upper Holloway / Hornsey Rise, London N19, his travels and observations are wide and varied. He has an opinion.

A trained operatic tenor, he is addicted to philosophical debate, wit and humour.

Would LOVE to have his own chat show!

an BeTter world

Memories of My Way!

Olympia Publishers
London

www.olympiapublishers.com
OLYMPIA PAPERBACK EDITION

Copyright © an BeTter world 2020

The right of an BeTter world to be identified as author of
this work has been asserted in accordance with sections 77 and 78 of the
Copyright, Designs and Patents Act 1988.

All Rights Reserved

No reproduction, copy or transmission of this publication
may be made without written permission.
No paragraph of this publication may be reproduced,
copied or transmitted save with the written permission of the publisher,
or in accordance with the provisions
of the Copyright Act 1956 (as amended).

Any person who commits any unauthorised act in relation to
this publication may be liable to criminal
prosecution and civil claims for damage.

A CIP catalogue record for this title is
available from the British Library.

ISBN: 978-1-78830-278-4

First Published in 2020

Olympia Publishers
Tallis House
2 Tallis Street
London
EC4Y 0AB

Printed in Great Britain

26.06.2025.

Here's to :—
Ethos — Pathos — Logos!

Dedication

I dedicate this book to ENERGY and all who may utilize it! said in her!

To Vernon!
Have A Great — FOREVER!
From
Bernie P.

Illegitimi non Carborundum!

Memories of My Way! — And The '60s! November/ December 1959

At 6.00 pm on Wednesday 11th November 1959 I experienced my first date with my first girlfriend, Georgina Dalmasio; she was a quarter Italian and I was soon to find out where that Latin quarter was!

Gina and I were attending the same school at Tufnell Park, London NW5. Her school, Burghley (probably named after Lord Burghley, the lifelong adviser of Elizabeth I), was a Secondary Modern School and had merged with my school, Acland Boys Central School, Fortess Road, London NW5, in the September of '59.

The apparent difference with the two schools was that Burghley was 'mixed' — boys and girls — whereas Acland was boys only. Having girls at school was quite a novelty for us Acland boys and many were attracted to that novelty, including myself.

I had no experience or confidence with girls, at the time. I was, and remained, an 'only child'. My closest relatives were all boys, the kids in the street were all boys, my friends at school were all boys. I was a boy and did what working class boys did in the 1950s — I played in the streets, with other boys!

Early on, in September, Georgina had already taken a shine to me. I recall, that a few House colleagues and I were in the playground, looking at photographs (black & white), taken at the previous Sports Day, in July 1959. Suddenly a head brushed against mine with a voice saying, "Nice pictures of you". It was Georgina!

I was in the 5th year of my secondary education, with the General Certificate of Education O Level Examinations looming fast upon me; due to be taken in the following summer, of 1960. Not that I was much of a scholar. The drone of the masters' voices sent me daydreaming; they were boring. How many sleepless nights did I endure, full of anguish and anxiety because I did not understand. Me, beating myself up, both mentally and emotionally, but all along it was the teachers' insensitivity. Why? Because they were boring and slow. I would start off understanding but then they would go off on a self-gratifying eulogy of nonsense. I have subsequently come to believe that those attracted to teaching are themselves frustrated actors and control freaks who need a captured audience to perform which, in effect, we kids were captive to. Then, after 10 years of captivity, I was summoned to the new headmaster's office (L.A.V. Abley), and summarily told that I was to take three G.C.E. O levels. Only three? What? No way! I politely reminded the headmaster that, at the tender age of fifteen, I was approaching the zenith of my educational career and now you want to deny me my opportunity? I walked out of his office with permission to take EIGHT O levels! My innate negotiating skills were beginning to emerge. And guess what? I subsequently proved him right! I passed only THREE O levels!

In addition to playing football for the school, I swam for the school, sang for the school and played basketball for the school. I was a brilliant dribbler of the ball and accurate basket scorer. In early November (1959) our basketball team played the Jewish Free School in Camden Road, between Camden Town and Holloway Road, where fifteen years earlier I was born, in the Royal Northern Hospital.

When we arrived at the Jewish Free School, Andy Adams, a Greek Cypriot friend, originally from Burghley School, told me that Georgina had arrived with a friend to watch me play basketball!

"What? Not me, must be Portch."

Dave Portch was in the basketball team and had, like me, graduated from Duncombe Road Primary School, London N19 to Acland Boys in September 1955, along with, Colin Croggon, Peter Fuzzey, Ronnie Passingham, Ronnie Poole and Harry Mead. Harry, ironically, not only being the person who passed over his early-morning paper round to me in February 1957, but also the second husband of Gina! The first? No! Not me. It was Vicky Long, also from the same class of 1954/55.

Portch was tallish, good looking, suave and confident with girls. "It must be Portch, not me," says I.

But Andy insisted that it was me she was after. I don't know why. At that time, I was not a dresser, I was not tall, I wasn't charming but I did have a great smile and friendly personality. Well, whether I believed it not, I played 'out-of-my-skin' during the match. I was 'inspired', driven by a force outside of my mortal body; I was flying, scoring basket after basket, many at the end of dazzling runs, including one from a corner. No one could touch me. All eyes were on me. It was a revelation!

Anyway, in the changing rooms, after the game, Andy comes in and tells me that Gina is waiting for me, outside. What? OMG! What am I going to do? What am I going to say? Well, I don't know how it happened but the next thing I remember was Gina and I standing together, outside the school, at the same trolley bus stop! It transpired that we both lived in the same Archway area of north London, N19. When the bus eventually arrived, I took the initiative to go upstairs to the top deck; I surmised that there would be less people up there, so more privacy, just in case, Gina and I would talk. Well, we did — talk! And I swear to God that I don't know how I did it, but I did — I asked Gina for a date — and she agreed! It was to be the following Wednesday, 11th November at 6.00 pm at the corner of Cressida Road and St. John's Way, diagonally opposite to my primary school, Duncombe Road, N19.

We met, somewhat awkwardly, but both on time. We then walked to the bus stop and caught the 210 single- decker bus to Finsbury Park. I had decided to take Gina to the Astoria Picture Palace (of latter Rainbow Rooms renown). The Astoria had originally been built in the 1920s when standards still meant something and were planned for practical usage, aesthetically designed and empathetically executed. Thus, as we, the courting couple — albeit Gina aged fourteen and me at fifteen — entered the foyer of the Astoria Picture Palace, we were enveloped by an ambience of pseudo-architectural grandeur.

Before us were Corinthian columns, marble floors, statues, water fountains, chandeliers, paintings, classical colours and decor. Gina and I must have appeared as a quaint spectacle against the backdrop of this pseudo-classical elegance. Two young teenagers, boy and girl, dressed in the emerging Italian styled clothes fashion. Me in my striped suit with a 'bum freezer' jacket, (short- short) and no turn-ups on my trousers! Gina in her short, pleated black skirt and tight white top which accentuated her amply grown, even at age fourteen, boobs! She wore a tatty woollen, fawn-coloured three-quarter length top coat, which did nothing for her figure, until she took it off!

After paying one shilling and six pennies (7.5 p) each, we were ushered by a courteous and helpful usherette into the auditorium, which was massive. I immediately noticed the star-studded ceiling, high above; it was romantic and exciting! Unfortunately, the coveted back row was already full; we had to make do with the fourth row down from the back, roughly in the middle. We sat down and that's when I felt excitement surge through my body. I knew that I was the one to do something but I wasn't sure what it was. I hadn't kissed a girl since Barbara Collins, when in the infants' school, still at Duncombe Road, eight years earlier, when I was seven years of age! I actually took her home to meet Mum and play cowboys and indians; doctors and nurses came later.

How do I get my arm around Gina and my lips on hers?

I pondered over the question for so long and so deeply that I transcended into visualization, which became — reality! I was sitting to the left of Gina (as Mr Bean does in his cinema sketch with his girlfriend) and have always taken my women from that side, ever since (especially whilst laying down).

Suddenly, my right arm was around Gina's shoulders, albeit somewhat awkwardly. However, she soon eased the awkwardness by sliding down the seat towards me. In this new position of potential, 'acquisition', one could have but one did not, touch the top of her right boob! Via my peripheral vision, I detected Gina looking towards my face, her head poised upward. BINGO! Like a rat out of a trap, my lips were firmly stuck on hers! I liked the sensation and so did she. So much so, that we continued to kiss until the end of the film — without a break! To the extent whereby when the lights came up, there was a round of applause from those seated in close proximity. In my naivety I thought the applause was for the enjoyment of the film until I heard such remarks as, "That's my boy!" "Let her come up for some air!" "What's this, a marathon?" I just said to Gina, "Would you like some ice-cream?" as the usherette passed the aisle with her tray of goodies. Then, into the second film and we were off again. My genitals were aching and — what was I going to tell Mum about my sticky underpants the next day?

A blur of memory, until it then crystalises with Gina and I locked in each other's arms, on the sheltered doorstep of her corner house of Harberton Road, N19. I knew I had to do something more. But what, without offending? I was desperately visualizing the female anatomy, especially Gina's. I wanted to be sure that when I made my move, I would hit bullseye, first time! I didn't even know what foreskin was, let alone foreplay. At that time, there was an unwritten etiquette that genitals should not be sought on the first date. However, dependent on mood, feelings, ambience and circumstances, the touching of boobs was acceptable, albeit with clothing in between. Apparently, I had created all four prerequisites, and grabbed a handful of silk blouse!

Memories of My Way!
1959

After an initial hiccup whereby I did not ask Gina for another date, I subsequently received a handwritten letter from her, via the post, a few days later, around the 22nd November. Can you believe that at fifteen years of age, in 1959, I received a perfectly handwritten letter from a fourteen-year-old girl! I'll never forget the occasion. Mum gave me the letter.

Mum: "I bet this is from your girlfriend." Mum was intensely intuitive — and interested.

Me: "Wha' for? Wha' she send me a le'er for?"

Mum: "I dunno — open it and see!"

Gina eloquently told me of her sadness and confusion in my non-follow-up date; she asked me if it was something she had done, or not done, and if it was the latter, then the remedy was readily available. Well, my oh my! Notwithstanding, the remedial process was soon readily enacted and enjoyed by both parties but, of course, not the 'Full Monty!' That was to come, next year, in 1960!

Gina and I would go for long walks around Parliament

Hill Fields, which was not far from where we both lived. Thus named, after the unsuccessful attempt to blow up the Houses of Parliament on the 5th November 1605 by Guy Fawkes (Dutch) and his Roman Catholic cronies. They climbed the hills, north of the city of London to witness and celebrate the blowing up of Parliament. Thus, the hills on which the cronies stood, were subsequently called Parliament Hill/ Fields. As a point of interest, the hills are part of an overall topography encompassing Hampstead Heath to the West and then to the East Highgate Hill, Hornsey Rise (where I grew up), Crouch Hill, Muswell Hill, which encompasses Alexander Palace where the BBC have a massive aerial to transmit signals for their various programmes. Furthermore, where cyclists commenced the Tour de Britain Cycling Tournament. Highgate Hill being of course of Highgate Village repute, whereby when turning left at the Spaniards Road, past Kenwood on the left, one eventually arrives at the Spaniards Inn, on the right. Adjacently opposite, across the narrow road, there is a brick/stone-built, one-storey building; more like a glorified shed where, as legend cajoles us to believe, Dick Turpin, the infamous highwayman, of the 18th century, hid from the law before his enduring ride to York!

Then, once through the bottle-neck, caused, primarily by the saviour of Dick Turpin (which has Preservation Orders for non-demolition), there is a straight road all the way to Jack Straw's Castle, the White Stone Pond and Hampstead Village.

When appropriate, Gina and I would stop for the exchange of personal favours: perhaps on a quiet bench seat, under a secluded tree or quite simply by lying on the grass — whatever! Our sexual explorations were becoming more erotic and daring — OMG! What will Mum say, when she finds out?

Christmas of '59 came and went; Gina and I were not together over the festive season. Mum and Dad had already arranged for us all to stay at the Megilley's in Camden Road, almost opposite the Jewish Free School where Gina and I shared our bizarre meeting just a few weeks before. Jack Megilley was one of Dad's first cousins from his mother's side of the family. He was short and stocky (like me), a powerful looking man (also like me), a copper-roofing foreman. His wife was tall and hospitable; they had produced three sons, John, Roy and Robert. Roy was a year younger than me, big, barrel-chested and fearsome. Ironically, he also attended Acland Boys, before merging with Burghley.

I think the merge rankled Roy's pride of Acland Boys School because he was forever beating up Burghley Boys! Roy had already established a reputation as a fighter before the merge with Burghley and before I knew that he was my second cousin. I think Roy considered Burghley to be low class, which, to be honest, it was, especially in comparison to the glory days of Acland and he vent his vengeance. However, not withstanding, he was eventually expelled from Acland-Burghley for beating a teacher to the floor! He didn't like the Burghley teachers, either!

As you can see, I come from good stock, also on my mother's side. A number of my older, maternal relatives had awaited Her Majesty's Pleasure for grievous bodily harm! But not me! The irony of Roy, however, was that although being expelled from school at age fifteen, he became for 25–30 years a main Board Director for Argos, previously Green Shield Stamps, in Edgeware, living in a pseudo mansion, in Oxfordshire.

Memories of My Way!
1960

I LOVE YOU! Those were the first words that I heard as 1959 ticked away into 1960; they were whispered softly, into my ear, by my girlfriend, Georgina Dalmasio. We were enjoying a New Year's party in a large terraced Edwardian house, basement an' all, in Tufnell Park Road, London N7, not far from our school. The party was being thrown by a girl, also fifteen years of age by the name of Carol. She adored one of my friends and classmates, Dave Gillard, who was also there. He was somewhat of the rocker's cult adorning the obligatory DA (Duck's Arse) Tony Curtis (albeit Bernie Schwartz) hairstyle.

This particular style of haircut, with his blond hair, was quite unusual and attractive to certain young girls at that time. Unfortunately, Dave was not attracted to her, Carol. Also, there was another good friend and classmate, Peter Roberts. He was there with a cute girl, petite, with ginger hair, also named Carol. They looked good together and well-suited. Pete was a brilliant artist, even before his tender age of fifteen. Not only brilliant in execution but also imagination; I was mesmerised by his artistic talent. He was instrumental in my attaining GCE O level in Art. Those examinations were to follow in the summer when educational qualifications meant something! I don't really remember much about the party, no doubt Gina and I spent it 'petting' but what I do remember was Carol, the hostess, repeatedly playing the Neil Sedaka top ten hit of the moment "Oh Carol!"

That was the 1st of January — the 31st was "Something Else!" (also a hit by Eddie Cochran).

The 31st of January 1960 was my first encounter of sexual intercourse; I was fifteen, Gina was fourteen!

The historical event was enacted in my attic bedroom in Calverly Grove, N19. You know what it's like, one thing leads to another and before you can say, 'Jack Robinson', it's ALL OVER! In this case, all over Georgina's midriff! I was so overcome with an unbelievable feeling of ecstasy, not previously experienced, that I cannot recall the exact mechanics of the event. What I do recall is that Georgina and I were well into a heavy petting session and that our genitals became magnetized towards each other. There was a compulsion of no turning back! It had to be! I recall simultaneous emotions of fear looming in my mind, furiously combating with a deep yearn and burn in my loins, the latter having now consumed my fear of 'what might happen, if'? My loins were aching from my continued endeavour not to ejaculate my sperm. But then the aching blended with a burning feeling of inexplicable pleasure as THE point of no return had come and my semen shot out!

When I emerged from the euphoria, the outcome was, thank God, everywhere. I had, somehow, employed coitus interruptus at some stage of this momentous occasion — but to what extent?

So, we waited, Gina and I; we waited — and we waited. What were we waiting for? Jane! Jane was the name Gina gave to her menstruation cycle. I don't know why but we began exchanging notes, filled with anxiety, worry and terror that she had not yet 'seen' Jane! A fourteen-year-old girl and a fifteen-year-old boy, alone, in an ocean of anxiety, in February/ March of 1960! Eventually the tension was not broken but changed, not in an ideal way but in a way that meant we were no longer alone in our ocean of anxiety; a rough 'life belt' was thrown, inadvertently, our way!

Gina's Mother had left her when she was a young girl, and like me, she was an only child. She lived with her Italian grandmother and her father who was a terrazzo contractor, travelling around the country. This meant that Gina was quite often on her own. However, there was a middle-aged female lodger who happened to find one of my naïve notes. On this discovery, she immediately took it upon herself to call on our house, a walking distance from Harberton Road N19 to Calverly Grove, N19, to share the news! I think Mum cried (perhaps, tears of joy) and Dad admonished me, primarily for putting 'something' in writing. I do not recall being severely reproached by either of my parents and there was no bitterness or animosity from them. We all squirmed for a few days more, contemplating the repercussions of Gina becoming pregnant, the thoughts appeared terrifying! But then, at last, Gina 'saw'

Jane and all were relieved. I recall saying something previously to Mum like, "We didn't go all the way!" This seemed to put her mind at rest because I distinctly remember her saying to my Dad, "'arry! He said they didn't go all the way!"

The outcome — upshot — of this traumatic experience was that I did not have sexual intercourse again, for two and a half years, when I was seventeen and a half!

Memories of My Way!
1960

Gina and I continued to see each other, in fact, most of the time but full sex for me was out of the question. I had learned my lesson! Furthermore, Mum and Dad had banned Gina and I from going to my attic bedroom, which, in retrospect, was a wise decision.

A few events occurred in the summer of 1960, notwithstanding taking my G.C.E. O levels and falling in love with Maria Bueno! Maria was a lady's tennis player, appearing at Wimbledon that year; I think she was Spanish but what I did know — she was beautiful! Probably the first female at Wimbledon to wear a short, white skirt, exposing small, tight frilly knickers. She had fantastic brown legs, strong hips and energetic boobs. Oh! I nearly forgot, and a great arse!

The catalyst between my new found 'love' and my REAL life was the intuitive brain of my mother. What did Mum do? She, out of the blue, bought me a tennis racket, albeit second hand, from a pawnbroker's in Hornsey Road. This racket and my new interest in tennis created a wedge between Gina and my friends, of whom I began to see more. For a short period of time my friends and I tried to improve our tennis skills, to the chagrin of Gina. I think she got jealous; eventually, we split physically but never, spiritually. Although petite, my mother was a clever strategist.

Another memorable event of the summer of '60 is of distinct note. I was on holiday with my good friend David Gillard, together with his mother and her boyfriend, in Raleigh, Essex. Dave and I had taken our pushbikes, albeit strapped to a car, but once there, we did cover a few miles cycling around the countryside; me with my Dawes Double Blue 10 gear, two flywheels (double) bike. Mum and Dad brought Gina down from London at the weekend. After a while Gina and I went for a walk along the lanes, alone. Soon we stopped by a field and laid down in the high corn, undetected. Before I could say, "How are you?" I was experiencing another first from Gina. She had slithered down my body and stopped — halfway! This time I had no reservations or restrictions and just let nature take its full course! OMG! I was now sixteen and Gina fifteen; where she got the idea from, I don't know but I was not complaining!

Summer of 1960

On leaving school I recall the last day at school. We were all dressed up in our finest clothes, maybe to show off to our colleagues/contemporaries/teachers and all and sundry!

I also recall Gina crawling around me — and I *was* tempted, I must admit, but I wanted change! Change of — everything! I wanted to grow up — fast!

The Careers Officer, situated in a dilapidated office near to Camden Town, was judgmental of me, due, I believe, to my Italian-style suit. He thought I was a yob and recommended that I become an apprentice to the heating and ventilating trade. When I told Dad, his foot went solidly down on the floor. No! Fortunately, with Dad, him being a bricklayer and knowing the work involved, in respect of heating and ventilating, did not want him participating in such a low-life trade.

It seemed that I had been categorized as a manual worker because the next option offered was as an apprentice toolmaker. When I told contemporaries, I was advised that it was a good job, with good money, after I had completed my indenture period of five years. A couple of Acland Old Boy names were dropped who worked there, which I recognized and that was it!

"What am I doing working in a factory?" I don't know. I didn't even get O level metalwork. Not because I didn't sit for it — I did, and failed! I was useless at it. Nevertheless, here I was, my first day at Ernest F. Moy & Co., Pratt Street, Camden Town, NW1, about to become an apprenticed toolmaker at GBP 4.4s.0d, / 84 shillings / 420 p, per week. And that was gross, before tax and national insurance contributions were deducted at source! I was ending up with something like GBP 3.15s.0d, for a forty-hour week! As an early morning paper boy, I was already earning GBP 1.13s.0d per week plus an additional 9s.6d from Mum, Dad and Nan for various weekly chores; Nan, my maternal grandmother, gave me 1s.6d per week, for getting up a pail of coal from the cellar, under the house every day. This meant that my current total income, as a schoolboy, was GBP 2.2s.0d! And this was for less than 10 hours each week. So, for an additional 30 hours per week, plus travelling time backwards and forwards from Hornsey Rise to Camden Town, I was only getting GBP 1.13s.0d! This was not financially attractive, to say the least, and I had to clock on, which I did not like, big time!

However, in 1960, work was about commitment, staying in the same job, learning a trade, becoming a foreman, making your work a career, so I persevered, with a good heart — to begin with.

Being the summertime, the older, longer-standing employees, were returning from their summer holidays. On three occasions I overheard them saying, one to another, "Another fifty weeks in this prison."

I was overcome by a feeling of claustrophobia because, yes! I *was* in a prison. "Let me outta here, I'm a Celebrity!"

My God, what am I going to do? (It was like a panic attack; I did not experience one of those until 1997, when I went from K.L., Malaysia to Tokyo, Japan). I took solace, standing at my lathe and capstan, singing, under my breath, inadvertently teaching myself breath control, which was particularly useful in later years when I took up singing seriously, bumping into opera along the way and culminating in an acceptance by Covent Garden in January 1975. The wife (an Australian dancer) of Alberto Remedios, England's renowned tenor, happened to hear me singing in Southgate, London N14. She subsequently introduced me to Alberto (a previous Liverpudlian ship-building welder who took on the Wagner Operas in the early 70s), who got me an audition at the English National Opera at St. Martin's in the Fields, near to, and north of, Trafalgar Square. I was subsequently introduced to one of ENO's vocal consultants, John/Jack Hargreaves, who tutored me and brought my voice on and up. I then wrote to Covent Garden, dropping a few names here and there and got the audition in January 1975. Although accepted after singing two arias, and to start work in six months' time in the chorus, I did not pursue. I loved/love singing, not acting. I got my satisfaction — I had been accepted by Covent Garden; that was good enough for me. What's next?

In the summer of 1960 Cliff Richard (Harry Webb) was hitting the charts with his group The Shadows, originally the

Drifters but there was a conflict of interest with Ben E. King (of *Stand by Me* fame) and his management because Ben E. King's backing group was also called The Drifters. Thus, the name, The Shadows, emerged as Cliff's backing group. Cliff, having been born in Lucknow, India, in 1940, came to England before he was ten years of age and eventually settled in Cheshunt, Herts, with his father working at Thorn's, the large electrical company on the A10 near to Enfield. In the early '70s I actually built an extension to a house that Cliff's sister, Jackie, had bought with her husband, Peter.

Cliff's second album, 'Cliff Sings', consisted, on the 'B' side, of many evergreen songs such as *As Time Goes By*. I memorized the words to the six evergreens so that I could sing them, ever so quietly, to myself, which gave me some solace in my new found prison!

However, I did make a new friend at Moy's, same age as me, sixteen, who was to become instrumental in my next female conquest during the summer of '61. His name, ironically, was Johnny Pratt. If you want to learn about 'front', meet Johnny Pratt. John was about my height, 5' 7" (on a good day) but half my width! He had an evil, satanic confidence, with hateful piercing eyes. He was tantamount to a 1960's Hitler! He had the ability to get men to follow him and his ideologies, which basically, was to cause trouble. I also was entranced by his demeanour and rhetoric. He appeared to know everyone that 'mattered' in Camden Town, Somers Town and King's Cross, also parts of the West End. He was lethal, uncompromising and unforgiving; a miniature Godfather with the connections and power to have most people apprehended, should he so desire.

I subsequently witnessed that power. He was born and bred in Camden Town, another only child. His parents were petrified of him!

I vividly recall an incident that occurred at the Ernest F. May Factory at Camden Town during the August of 1960.

Every morning, ladies with trolleys would come up to the men working at the lathes and capstans, etc., with mugs of tea and great cheese and ham rolls. After I bought my refreshment, I had developed a habit of finding a spot close by to sit down and enjoy my deserved nourishment. I remember on one occasion the foreman approaching me and saying,

"What do you think you are doing?"

"Drinking tea and eating rolls," was my curt, honest and logical retort.

"You can't do that! You can't stop work! Eat at the lathe!"

"You want me to stand up, at the lathe, eating and drinking and STILL work? No! I'm not doing that. That's dirty and dangerous!"

The foreman walked off in amazement and astonishment. That was the final straw — for me!

I was BERNARD TETLOW; I was sixteen and I already knew I could earn money outside of that prison!

I told my parents what had happened, and my dad just couldn't believe it. He had been a bricklayer all of his life, working on various and numerous sites, but had never encountered such barbarism. With this current news of 'factory-style tea breaks', Dad was infuriated and asked me the £64,000 question, "What are you doing to do now?" Answer:

"Go back to school!" I had already given the situation a lot of thought. I needed to get my head straight on what I REALLY wanted to do. Fortunately, I had not signed the apprentice toolmaker Indenture Contract, so I was FREE to go! I had procrastinated to sign because I was not happy and, now I was about to have the pleasure of telling the foreman what to do with his job. He was aghast when I told him I was leaving. "What about your money?" he enquired.

I said, "You can send it on, if you like. I can earn more money as a paper boy and go back to school!" I just walked out of prison!

But now, I had to act fast! Number one, I had to get my three paper rounds back ASAP — and I did! Because I had been working at Ernest F. Moy for only six weeks, ironically the same duration of the school summer holidays, the owner of the paper shop had not had time to find anyone to replace me. Furthermore, I had been working for him regularly and conscientiously since February 1957. It was now September 1960 and during those three and a half years I had taken over three paper rounds as the other boys left; that's why I was earning so much money. And, I never took ONE day off!

Next, I had to get back to school and persuade the headmaster that I needed more education. I had seen the light and the error of my ways. It was particularly satisfying when he agreed because I, like most other boys at Acland Central Boys School, latterly known as Acland Burghley, didn't like him. He was a prick! Ya! That's it. L.A.V. Abley was his name; what an idiot he was. The complete antithesis of our previous headmaster, Mr Pearson, more affectionately referred to as 'Tapper' because he was tactile with us boys, invariably tapping us on our heads. He was an 'old school' headmaster — a disciplinarian and fair; a caring man of principle and understanding. He was big and a born leader of men. He always wore pinstripe trousers, a black waistcoat with a white shirt and silver tie plus a lightweight three-quarter length cut away 'frock'-type black top coat. We boys were so fortunate to have a headmaster like Tapper. We ALL loved him because he CARED! Anyway, Abley let me come back to school which, in retrospect, I believe, was an unusual decision, albeit an unusual request. I went back to take two more G.C.E. O levels in English and Maths, at the Christmas sitting, which I got. Wonders will never cease! Remember, Abley was the one I had persuaded to allow me to take eight O levels previously, in the summer sitting? Even at sixteen I was quite verbose, especially when it was a matter of principle. I think I inherited it from Mum. I was brought up that way to respect and stick up for myself. I saw myself as a cheeky little sod- and I still do. I love that self-image. I think Abley was afraid of what I might say next or what I might even do next. It was probably on record that Mum had previously been up to the school, in person, to admonish a teacher, Chapman, the woodwork teacher, in public for caning the backs of my legs, causing the skin to come up in welts (no long trousers then), for no bad reason. Furthermore, that a cousin of mine, Roy, had been expelled from school for punching a teacher to the ground. (Subsequently to become a director of Green Shield Stamps and the director of Argos.) Abley got scared — he succumbed.

Within six weeks, I had travelled 360 degrees. But, within

those six traumatic weeks I had learned much about life. My experiences had given me a confidence to push my adolescent naivety far beyond the status quo. I was maturing — fast! I had grown, emotionally!

I was BERNARD TETLOW and I was sixteen years of age!

MY WAY!

September to December went by soon enough with me passing GCE O level (General Certificate of Education), in English and RSA (Royal Society for Arts) in Arithmetic. I now had a total of three O levels in English, Art and History plus one RSA in Arithmetic. However, throughout my life, I have never been asked once, for evidence of their existence, or of them being of any significance. Having said that, I suppose when applying for a job as a bricklayer, bus driver or milkman, qualifications are not the first thing that spring to the mind of the prospective employer.

As 1960 drew to a close I racked my brain as to what career path I should take. I was still playing regular football but had given up on my pipe dream of becoming a professional footballer. A footballer's lifestyle was quite precarious and grossly underpaid in 1960. Furthermore, if a professional footballer sustained a significant injury at that time, the chances were that their career would be over. Not only did they not get the money they deserved, neither did they get the medical treatment they deserved; not like the balloon-kickers of today. One twisted ankle and they are off the pitch, out of the match and on the missing list for who knows how long, to be seen, sometime later, in the early hours of the morning, in an expensive night club!

When it happened, I can't exactly recall when the 'penny dropped', from my sub-conscious to my conscious mind. But the catalyst to which I do recall, was Mum saying, when I was a kid, years before.

"'Ere, guess what? That bleedin' insurance bloke's got a car now! How do they do it? They start off with a pushbike, then they get a motorbike — now, he's got a bleedin' car! There's something in this insurance game!"

This recollection of mine was of the mid-1950s, living in Fairbridge Road, London N19, before we moved to Calverley Grove, N19, in 1958.

That was it! I knew what I wanted to be and do. I wanted to be an insurance agent. It smelt of money. I also felt the 'freedom and independence'. I knew that the insurance man had a round and called on people; I already had a round — a paper round. I could identify with the basics of what the insurance man was doing. He called on people to collect money (insurance premiums), I knew that much. The thoughts felt good! I can do that! He also made my mum and grandmother laugh, he had personality. People had told me that I had personality. I didn't know quite what that was, but I knew it was verbal and made people laugh. That's what I wanted to do, to make people laugh; it was already, in me.

Quite often Mum and Nan would admonish the insurance man in a jocular way by making such comments as: "You cheeky sod, get back on your bike." (That's when he had a bike; when he had a car, the meaning was more metaphorical.) I liked that; I liked people saying that to me. I liked, nay loved, being cheeky; maybe because Mum was cheeky. She had bundles of personality and could make people laugh. She was also argumentative and confrontational; she got that from the genes of her father and the actions of her mother, who loved to argue and fight; and so did the brothers of her husband, my maternal grandfather.

So, I wanted to be an insurance agent, but I had one big problem, a real problem. Although I was still Bernard Tetlow, I was also still, ONLY sixteen!

"Whatever the mind can conceive and believe, it can achieve!"

I told my parents about my aspirations of becoming an insurance agent. All I got back was: "Let's wait and see!"

Anyway, somehow or other, at the commencement of 1961, I managed to secure a position with A. J. Collins & Co., a reinsurance company in Leadenhall Street, in the City of London. Well, it had the word insurance in it; what the pluck reinsurance was, I had no idea. And although (I had waited, and I had seen) there was no guidance from home when it came to a career path, Mum loved me to bits and Dad was always in work and a responsible father, there were no plans or discussion about my career path. I think I must have gone back to the same careers officer in Camden Town, of my own volition. I didn't know what else to do. And even though I had already turned down one of his recommendations and walked out of the other, he still helped me. I shared my insurance agent aspirations with him and he referred me to a careers officer in the City of London. I had never been to the City before, even though I lived only four–five miles away, at Upper Holloway, in the Borough of Islington. I was naturally nervous, so I cajoled Dad to accompany me. The interview was in the afternoon but Dad would not take time off work. So, at the age of 48 he climbed up the high hoarding surrounding the Cancer Research Laboratories, (Lincoln's Inn Fields, Holborn, west of the City of London) building site and jumped down the other side. Little did I know that this very same site would be instrumental in my future career path, before the end of 1961.

Dad and I travelled by underground train from Holborn to the City. Eventually we found the address and there I was, confronted by a 1960/61 City Slicker-style man. His dress reminded me of 'Tapper', (our beloved Headmaster) pinstripe trousers an' all. He was an OK fella and subsequently offered me an interview as a clerk, at A.J.Collins in Leadenhall Street for the princely sum of GBP 6.10s.0d per week. I showed interest and he made an appointment for me to attend. I went alone and got the job! And Dad wasn't missed on site; we met up later, at home.

I was to commence my duties as an office clerk after the 1960 Christmas festivities. I wasn't exactly excited, but I had to start somewhere and I liked the idea of GBP 6.10s.0d a week plus three shillings / 15 pence per day for luncheon vouchers.

The dress code in the City of London had probably not changed for fifty plus years with top hats and bowlers compulsory, for those of high standing. It seemed that all clothing was of a black and white combination. But here was I in this new-fangled Italian style clothing of varying colour and design; not black or white. OMG!

By the age of sixteen, I had personally purchased, with my own money, three Italian-style suits. The first one I bought was at age fifteen, off-the-peg. It was of woollen material, black vertical stripes on a grey background. I had the jacket shortened and the turn-ups to the trousers taken out as an endeavour to conform to the Italian style. My next suit I had made to measure at N. Berg Tailors, Caledonian Road, London N1. That's the road that leads from Holloway to King's Cross

A friend of mine, Dave Portch (the prefect with whom I had fought, and which caused me to become a hero within my own tea-break, circa 1954/55; more of that later), was now a fashion freak. He advised me about style, colour, material, jacket lapel width, pocket flap depth, cuff buttons, zip fly, etc., etc. I chose a Prince of Wales check material with an overall greyish colour effect. The jacket was cut to double-breasted style, with bum freezer length — short! It cost me 15 guineas — GBP 15.15s.0d, 15 pounds and 15 shillings, which, at that time in 1960, was quite a sum, especially for a school boy with a paper round! I was, or thought I was, the 'cat's whiskers', albeit, 'Jack the Lad!' or more latterly, 'the dog's bollocks'!

The next suit I bought, also made to measure and at the same tailor's, was somewhat, over the top. It was a dark brown, of a woollen material, cut to a single-breasted style with a distinctly under-classed, curving cut-away (of the corners to the jacket) to the base of the jacket, albeit of my design. That one cost me GBP 16 guineas, even though it was less material!

In the City of London, during January 1961, I must have stood out like a sore thumb!

Memories of My Way! 1961

Memories of A.J. Collins are somewhat blurred and mediocre. I recall reams and reams of paperwork; no one really telling me what I should do, no line management. I was bored — big time! No one ever checked on me or spoke to me; I was actually, doing nothing.

But what I do, vividly, remember was that all employees referred to the directors as 'Sir'. I had vowed to myself that when I left school my days of calling people sir, were over!

The other employees told me, "You must call the directors, Sir!"

"Why?" I replied.

"Because they pay your wages," the answer came back.

"Yes, for me to be here; they pay me for my time."

The silence was deafening. I was somewhat ostracized for that. So, what's new?

I was still sixteen. They got me delivering the post to the individual directors; I think there were three. I used to say... "Good morning, Mr Tom, Dick and Harry!" (Not so many dogs in offices in those days.) More often than not I would get a smile back. I felt an affinity with them — the directors. What most employees don't understand is that to have your own successful business you have to be a bit of a maverick! You need to be a leader and not a follower. You need to be able to think on your feet — out of the box. You need 'intelligent ignorance' the quality referred to in my book *Tetlow (FMS) hsb 13.6.18: Choose to Change!* I think the directors felt my streak of independence and individuality; maybe because of my dress style. I was ignorant of what people thought because I couldn't care less but intelligent enough not to be interested in anything for which I saw no value or no challenge, no reward, albeit financial, physical or intrinsic. Sure, I was polite but not subservient!

I recall a strange ritual that I had developed towards the latter stages of my association with A.J. Collins. It would occur on a Friday afternoon, soon after I had been paid, minus what the government wanted, of course. I would go to the toilet, sit on the seat fully clothed, take the money out of my pocket and throw the pound notes and ten shilling notes up in the air and then watch them fall to the ground! Then, contemplating the time and effort made by me to be at A.J. Collins against the pieces of paper floating to the floor, I wasn't happy. In fact, I was unhappy! I was not inspired, motivated or challenged.

However, my social life was becoming increasingly active. I was now playing football for two teams, Saturday afternoons and Sunday mornings. I was seeing more of Johnny Pratt, mainly at dance halls in central London. He was always looking for confrontation and the opportunity to be anti-social in some way; it was like he had a chip on his shoulder about something.

The highlight of my week was going to the Tottenham Royal Dance Hall when the Dave Clark 5 were playing there, before they become famous.

Just to give you a feel and taster of the musical ambience, Jeff Rowena was the alternate, resident band. There were two important elements of knowledge of life that I learned by going to the Tottenham Royal:

1) Females prefer bold males
2) The enlightening effects of alcohol.

Going to dance halls on a regular basis, introduced me to alcohol. Previously I had experienced one-off bouts of drinking, like Carol's New Year's party 1959-60. Also, birthday parties, special occasions and, of course, Christmas. I had been a big drinker as a kid — non-alcoholic, of course. I could drink a pint of milk straight down ever since I can remember, kept cool in a bucket of cold water, no refrigerators then; well, not for the likes of us. Water, orange juice, lemonade, barley water and cider; I loved cider (is cider alcoholic?). You name it and I could drink volumes of it. I had an insatiable thirst — and still do, except for Guinness. Up to the age of eleven, when I was on school holidays, every Friday lunch time I would be with my mum and grandmother, in her small, 'kitchened range' kitchen, eating real, glorious fish 'n' chips with them drinking Guinness. I tried a sip on a number of occasions but could not get my taste buds around it. On draught — well now, that's a different world!

One off, impact drinking was okay and I enjoyed it but I

always ended up with a headache the next day. But what I found, albeit over a period of years, with regular drinking, was that I built up like an immune system to headaches and sickness. Furthermore, the alcohol caused me to feel tranquil, creative and talkative. It seemed to release an intellectual energy force within me, of which I was unaware. It caused me to become more of the person I wanted to be. It seemed to clarify my thinking. Fortunately, it also transpired that I had a strong threshold against intoxication. Fortunately, also was my ingrained self-discipline and self-respect. I was not about to be drunk or seen to be drunk. In fact, my brain became clearer and sharper. My tongue seemed to have a new and faster connection with my brain. I was speaking a mini second after my mind had assimilated my thought processes. My retorts, on any subject, were spontaneous. As time went by, I challenged myself to out talk anybody about anything; sometimes three or four people at a time. I was like a verbal samurai swordsman, lashing my tongue in all directions. Sometimes it got me in hot water but I didn't care — I was having fun! I loved to be cantankerous but not confrontational. I enjoyed the exquisite mental gymnastics to which I thrust myself and the resulting flowing of words. It was magical because I had no conscious choice of words. I felt as if I had been tuned-in to a piece of sophisticated — 'something' — or somebody! I am extremely sensitive to atmospheres, vibes, and body language. I was now capitalizing on my sensitivity by verbalizing my feelings and observations. This new-found skill augured well for my future addiction in life — SELLING! But I must admit, I'm still not as good as those politicians and religious people! Yeah! They got me beat man! 'With God on your side — how can you lose?'

So here I am, at just seventeen, creating the self-image of the kind of person I wanted to be. But I knew that 'devil's brew' would consume me faster than I could consume it. And so, because I had respect for myself, I had respect for the negative potential of the effects of excessive drinking.

There was a history of adverse drinking on both sides of my family. I recall that during one of my inquisitive moods, when I was about ten years of age, I was persisting with my grandmother to tell me about her family, by the name of Everard. I frequently teased her about the name, much to her chagrin. She used to chase me upstairs calling me a cheeky little sod. Anyway, she taught me how to play Ludo, Snakes and Ladders, dominoes and various card games. I learned chess in my secondary school and could complete Solitaire (one peg in the middle hole) when I was about eight or nine. She eventually revealed to me one day that her father had been a licensee and died of alcoholism.

On my dad's side, I remember him telling me how he and his elder sister and older brother used to wait in the dark and the cold for their parents to return home from drinking at the Plimsoll Pub in St. Thomas' Road, Finsbury Park N4. This is the long road that leads from the Finsbury Park bus, train and underground terminal to the Arsenal Underground Station. The only football club with its name on a station! I remember going to see Cliff Richard at the Finsbury Park Empire, which, at the time, was at the top of St. Thomas' Road — it's a mosque now!

Memories of My Way! 1961

The other important piece of knowledge that I acquired by frequenting dance halls was that females like bold males. How many times did my friend Colin and I go to dance halls, full of 'spunk' and optimism that we were going to 'pull' that night (get a girl) to inevitably find ourselves catching the last bus home alone, again! We would approach girls on the periphery of the dance floor, asking them to dance.

"Would you like to dance?"
"No, thank you!"
"Would you like to dance?"
"No, thank you!"

Please try to imagine that in 1961, girls and boys were different; to be more precise, the social etiquette between males and females, was different from today. There were still overtones of Victorianism lurking in the sub-conscious, albeit loitering, ready to emerge at the most awkward occasions. But we, Colin and I, were of the new, bold and brave, generation. We would cast fear, humiliation, and embarrassment aside. It took courage to walk up to a strange girl in public and invite rejection! However, as with most endeavours in life, when one has endeavoured enough times, one adjusts. So, I got used to "No, thank you!" and used it as a source of fun. To prove the point of how robotic the retort of "No, thank you!" was, I would walk up to a likely candidate, open my mouth, pause and before any sound could come out, I would hear, "No, thank you!" That's when I deduced that I was not the recipient, personally, of "No, thank you!" "No, thank you!" was the hackneyed retort of certain girls. They had decided to employ, "No, thank you!" as a 'cop out' not to expose their own, fragile egos.

So, I used empathy to get to the bottom of it. Maybe...

1) She can't dance!
2) She's nervous, shy!
3) She didn't want to be teased by her friends!
4) It's 'cool' to reject a man in the presence of her peers!
5) Procrastination is 'safe!'

When all of these 'pennies' dropped into place and I realized that, "No, thank you" was not a personal rebuff to me, my confidence level rose.

So how can Colin and I get more girls at dance halls?

Because in 1961, that was the only place you could find the fair sex. Well, at least for us working-class proletariat. The next challenge was, where to take them. Up against a wall was never my style, especially in the winter. Although if one did, nature would cause the jolly old 'knee-wobbles'. Do you remember that 'ol boy?

With the coming of the mid to late 1950s, the working

class began to buy motor cars (short for carriages). At last a convenient and mutually accepted 'venue' was found for members of the opposite sex to indulge in sexual promiscuity. Enter my contemporaries and me. However, still not ideal, especially in small cars, unless you had a heater and reversing light. Positions did improve with the advent of seat belts which neatly provided a practical resting place for the female's ankles, who by this time would be on the back seat. WARNING! Not recommended for small ladies in wide cars! We, in the working class socio-economic 'section' of society were not accustomed to visiting hotels and no motels then. I think I was twenty-eight years of age when I first stayed in a hotel and that was organized and paid for by the company I was working with at the time. Going back to one's pad was also out of the question because at that time, young people lived at home with their parents until they got married. No point waiting for parents to go out, go for a drive or go on holiday to grab some privacy for fun and games; parents stayed in at home. At that time, it was not deemed cool to hock oneself up to the eyeballs with indebtedness. If you couldn't pay for it, then you went without. The inevitable outcome of this frugality was that most families stayed at home, engaging themselves in recreational hobbies and pastimes. However, the breakthrough commodity (toy) which broke this financial self-control was the automobile (then bricks and mortar). I bought one when I was seventeen, I wasn't good at Maths but I was good with calculating money, especially when interest rates were concerned, albeit simple or compound. (Keep away from that compound stuff.) I knew how to get a settlement figure from a hire purchase company when I was 18, plus concessionary reductions.

Times were about to change — big time! Just as Bob Dylan predicted in 1965. Yes! Math<u>S</u>, with an '<u>S</u>' please. Maths is an abbreviation of Mathematics which is plural. When a word is abbreviated it must maintain its basic meaning. I can show you a set of Mathematics but can you show me a Math?

Memories of My Way — And the 60's!
1961

Work trudged on at the offices of A.J. Collins in the City of London. I began to develop the habit of dreaming, creating and planning ahead!

"Long-term goals overcome short term frustrations!"

Out of curiosity and a desire to experience new horizons, I decided to see more of Johnny Pratt. We arranged to holiday in Jaywick Sands, Clacton-on-Sea, Essex, with a gang of hooligans, from Camden and Somers Towns, in the summer of '61. The experience turned out to be anything but a holiday! I got to Jaywick by train, on my own. We all met up and shared two chalets. The first event I recall was John intimidating a family in the next chalet to lend us their car, a Hillman Minx. They were too scared to turn John down, and of course, the inevitable happened. Whatever the purported experience of the allocated driver from the gang may have been, he promptly crashed the car; almost a write off! The police got involved and we all quickly 'vamoosed'! What was I doing here?

I also recall that at some stage I found myself in bed with

two girls and one boy! The layout was, boy, girl, girl, boy. I was one of the boys (crowd laughs out loudly!). I can't remember the appearance of the girl but I know she was a girl because... Well, something must have happened because when I awoke in the morning, part of my anatomy was outside of my clothing and all around was damp and sticky! Ah! Those were the semen days of my youth. "They seek it here, they seek there, those free-wills seek it everywhere!" (Ooh! I do hope I'm not being politically, incorrect.)

We all moved into two other chalets in a different area. John organized everything as usual and ironically, the chalets were better. He had a knack of persuading people of a variety of walks of life to obey his will — but not girls; he had no confidence with females of a contemporary age.

My next recollection is that of us all drinking milk, at King John's instructions, to line our stomachs before going out on a bender. We drank in the chalets before we went out. Then we drank here, we drank there, we drank everywhere! We ended up in a club somewhere — I think. Most of the social evening remains hazy, as you would expect. But what does remain crystal clear was the scenario that followed as we left the club and onto the street. There, before us, was a gang of up to ten local 'hounds' about to attack the five of us. They had the surprise effect and it became a free-for-all — every man for himself! I remember my fists and feet making contact with whom or what I knew not. And then, we made a run for it. I was on my own and running down a long side street. Suddenly, I was aware of a car head-beam on my back, exposing my whereabouts. The engine of a car roared! The horn blasted!

What the pluck! Before I knew it, I was over the low front gate of the next house on the right. I heard dogs barking. I smashed through the wooden door to the back garden and raced over the lawn, then over the low dividing garden wall and onto the lawn of the house opposite, through the garden fence door, alongside the flank wall of the house and into the front garden, over the gate and into the road. I ran as fast as I could down the road when suddenly a field appeared on the right with long grass. I ran along the path for a couple of minutes and then jumped into the grass and waited.

I waited and I waited, for about twenty minutes but nothing happened. Eventually I got up, and at that point I realised I had pain coming from all over my body; bruises, cuts and blood. I somehow managed to find my way back to the chalets. Some fellas were already there, others drifting in from time to time. No one had a serious injury and no one knew what actually happened — it was all so quick. However, the overriding factor was that (King) John was not a happy bunny; he was embarrassed and MAD! Satisfaction MUST be HAD!

I don't know how he did it but during the course of the next day, John got through to other London gangs in Clacton-on-Sea and persuaded them to meet up and join us in search of the perpetrators of our humiliation. Eventually we all met, and I recall some 'heavy' names that permeated 'Our Manor' of North/North West London. Names that, the utterance of which would instil fear into the minds of most contemporaries. Having said that, not the top echelon of the hooligan element trading in London at that time, like the Kray Brothers in East London.

John had also managed to find a 'grapevine' to send a message to the leader of the local gang, to meet up; to give him his due, he obligingly turned up, albeit with his gang behind him. However, he was not expecting to be confronted by a much larger and ferocious set of thugs than the last encounter. This time, the tables were reversed as we had now grown to nearly twice their numbers; in effect, we surrounded them in a circle. John walked up to the six-foot leader with the aplomb of a Roman General about to humiliate his vanquished foe. John was oozing confidence, he was in his element, upright, with venom in his eyes; his stature grew. The six-footer, however, seemed to shrink and his demeanour was that of a vanquished foe, with his tail between his legs, ready to fall to his knees and accept his punishment. John seemed to double in size when he was mad; a seasoned psychopath. He exuded controlled manic power. He loved confrontation and revelled in his natural ability to intimidate other males. John was now well within the 18" comfort zone of his now quivering adversary, burning hatred via his cold, satanic eyes, into those of his victim who quickly looked away. John's performance of projecting evil intentions was awesome! Of course, our superior numbers supported him but nevertheless his oratory was spine-chilling. At 5'7", weighing in at less than ten stone, John had developed, mastered and polished the art of psychological intimidation. He had an unusually deep and powerful voice and had created the weird habit of burping, extremely loudly; it was like his signature. He could do it at will and employed it at certain psychological moments to create uneasiness and to be used as a closing gesture of confirmation to get what he wanted. i.e. "Got it?" Buuuuuuurrrp!

I recall John threatening the gang leader with pain if there was any possibility of more trouble. He, John, would organise an army of thugs, maimers and killers, albeit dropping more names of persons of ill repute who would come down from London and take them out completely. And he, the leader, would be put on trial by selected thugs, found guilty and then tortured both mentally and emotionally. After which he would be taken to a place of facilitation in London, stripped naked then beaten, belt and chain whipped, his testicles placed in a vice and squeezed to a pulp. Then taken to Epping Forest and left alone, to rot! The victim was on the verge of collapse, ashen faced, trembling, unable to speak. John pushed his face into the face of fear and released an enormous burp. "Buuuuuurrrp! Got it?" The head nodded in agreement; there was no more trouble. King John prevailed!

Memories of My Way — And the 60's!
1961

The following Saturday we decided to throw a party. It was about time we got some GIRLS! We were all delegated our respective duties by King John. My responsibility was to supply the music. In retrospect and to the chagrin of my parents, I had brought a few of my records on holiday with me from my beloved record collection, which proved to be a mistake. I had started my collection in February 1957 when I became an early morning paper boy.

During the Saturday afternoon a few of the bolder members of our motley crew went from Jaywick Sands into Clacton-on-Sea, to 'pull' girls to come along to the party. I remember that I commenced the music quite early, at around 7.00 pm. On arrival I was to entertain the girls with my effervescent personality, scintillating conversation and imbue them with alcohol.

At this juncture of my brief interest in fashion, I wore detachable collar shirts. I had a variety of collars, all white. Some were pointed, some rounded and also a 'flyaway' version; usually seen in the Victorian era. I loved them because they were different and created the impression that I had a neck! That evening I wore my blue collarless shirt (exactly the same as shirts worn by policemen, at that time) and one of my rounded white stiff collars. At seventeen I had developed and continued to develop a muscular body, the outline of which could be observed by my close-fitting shirts, especially with the advent of Ben Sherman shirts. Girls began to drift into the chalet. I was still somewhat apprehensive towards females and was not good at small talk. As they walked in, I smiled and served them drinks. No one took my eye until... 'Brigitte Bardot' (Camille Javal) walked in! OMG! (Oh, my God!) She was absolutely beautiful. I could not believe my eyes. A sixteen-year-old B.B., oozing sex appeal from every inch of her body: her face, eyes, shoulders, boobs, waist, butt, legs. And guess what? She was looking at me — especially. Such a sexy and seductive smile coming 'My Way!' I felt, right there, that I was the 'Chosen One'. Her gaze was magnetic and mesmerising, demanding and controlling. This girl was experienced, powerful and she knew what she wanted. She looked at me and saw that which she wanted. (My stiff — collar!) I became a little nervous that I may not be able to satisfy her needs. But I was willing to try! My body churned and quivered from head to toe. Something was stirring and yelling at me. Yes! She wants YOU! Take her! But how? This was a new scenario for me, more adult, not playground stuff. OMG!

"Excuse me, would you like a drink?"

Who said that? I looked around — nobody there. It must

have been me. "Yes, please. What have you got?"

For you darling — Aaaaarrrh!

"Come over and have a look." (Who is this bold bastard?)

My God is this really me talking to Brigitte Bardot? Will I actually pluck her — feathers?

Memories of My Way!
1961

Her voice was so cute, seductive and alluring. Brigitte was definitely different from the regular girl of 1961 — she was bold and unabashed. She let me know from the expression in her eyes that and her body language that she was 'up for it' and that I was her chosen prey for the night — ASAP!

We shared a couple of drinks and innuendo chit-chat to confirm our lust for each other; we both had 'ants in our pants' making her itchy, and me horny, to fuck each other. As the seconds dragged by, we both grew more and more impatient to have sex! As we drew close, I put my arms around her lower back and pulled her even closer into my lower torso. Her eyes opened wide as she felt my thumping hammer; her pouting lips parted as a sub-conscious gesture of willingness and submission. As I squeezed this goddess to my chest, did I feel boobs? I felt BOOBS!

With her bolster of boobs, her big blue eyes, cute nose, golden blond hair and full, pouting lips, strong hips and great arse, my muscular body, thumping hammer and powerful clench around her waist, we just couldn't wait any longer! There were three bedrooms leading off the main lounge/dining/kitchen area, whereby now, everyone was congregating. I sensuously gazed into her also sensuous eyes with both expressions silently confirming our lust for each other. It was hot and animalistic! I turned my head to one of the bedroom doors, simultaneously flicking my eyebrows in the same direction. I returned my eyes to hers and raised my eyebrows. She nodded in approval. I could still not believe what was happening. Was I actually going to 'pluck' this young goddess?

YES, I WAS GONNA PLUCK this young goddess!

We sloped off from the maddening crowd as inconspicuously as possible. I envisaged kicking off with some foreplay, like kissing and cuddling. You know what I mean 'arry?

I was not expecting what actually happened, so fast. As soon as the door closed, she was at me. She jumped at me, opening her legs in mid-air, then clasping her arms around my neck and legs around my waist on impact, nearly knocking me over. Then she threw her head backwards, causing me to fall forwards, off balance and onto the bed! When I fell on top of her she gasped as my masculinity pressed onto her femininity. She seemed to love the weight of my body on her hers as an emotion and gesture of complete submissiveness, of her femininity to my masculinity. 'I'm yours, to do with as you want!'

Our hands were everywhere in a frenetic impatience to rid ourselves of the remainder of our clothing. At last we were naked, laying together with our skin lightly touching, exploring, in wonderment, at the beauty of our young bodies. I was seventeen, she sixteen. We simultaneously slid our fingers along the surface of our bodies. Her skin was as smooth as velvet and adorable to kiss and lick. She took hold of my rocket (soon to be launched) so delicately and lovingly, then slid down for final preparation. OMG! There was a premature 'lift-off' but she was brave and took the initiative by consuming the outcome to reduce exterior inconvenience; for which I truly appreciated and admired her! Now I was determined to 'whip-up' her cream pot! Not only was Brigitte so beautiful, sexy and desirable, but also so clean, with a seductive aroma; 'finger-lickin' good!' But fingers were not enough for this sex goddess — she was gonna get something more! I felt compelled to taste her source of divinity — her pot of cream and enjoy the journey down, from head-to-tail, via her Milky Way! I slowly kissed, licked, sucked and nibbled my way down her tempting body, starting with her delicate neck then down to her upper chest (didn't stay there for long), on to her amazing firm, kick-up boobs and suckable button nipples, which she insisted I bite, until I tasted iron! She squealed with pain and pleasure and her hips rose upwards as the sensation communicated with her pussy. Then down onto her soft, flat belly, stopping to twirl the tip of my tongue inside her navel and sucking hard on her umbilical knot as a gesture of erotic intent. Down through the aroma of her Palmolive soap-smelling foliage and then finally arriving at the entrance of her immensely desirable cream pot! She gasped and let out a quiet groan of pleasure as my tongue flipped the top of her lid. Her body stiffened and arched as her legs parted to allow my adventurous master-key to unplik her plock! She was — yummy! She abruptly jerked my head deeper into her — her! The palms of her hands about my ears and fingers spread tightly at the back of my head (she had big hands), thrusting my head on and off her — her! I was developing immaculate timing, just to breath. At the crescendo of her gyrations she gave out an enormous scream and buried my head into her — her!

My two upper front teeth, which have a gap, were either side of her clitoris (big gap — small clit)! I could flick it with my tongue at the back of my teeth. Extracting it was fun, also painful and somewhat pleasurable for Brigitte. When it eventually popped out, we both roared with laughter.

Brigitte had experienced multiple orgasms with a culminating massive orgasm at the end. Furthermore, as I was about to learn, she was insatiable — she wanted more. So, she took the bit between her teeth and chewed and chewed and chewed until there was very little left to chew. Still not satisfied, she now craved the Full Monty. Memories of 31st January 1960 came rushing to the forefront of my mind but again, temptation got the better of me. Here I am with a young Greek goddess on her knees reciprocating my oral performance gazing up at me with — 'please' exuding from her whole persona; subliminally urging me to enter her pathway to ecstasy. Now laying on top of her beautiful sixteen-year-old, hot body, pulsating beneath me; it would be rude to deny her. So, I succumbed and took up her alluring invitation to visit her 'charms'.

I slid through into her slippery orifice into the velvet-layered passageway until I reached the end. The velvet texture subtly and in a clingy way, caressed both my latitude and longitude. Brigitte's eyes popped wide and stared upwards, her jaw fell loose, and she began to pant as she felt my size. She placed her hands firmly on my shoulders to thwart further penetration. We lay still, in a state of inertia, both subconsciously contemplating whether we should try further penetration. We both wanted to experience the limits. Brigitte tweaked my shoulders with her fingers as a sign to try! I stoked up a head — of steam, to return to a state of momentum. As I eased along her passageway, I believed that I was now approaching unchartered folds of velvet because Brigitte grimaced with new and unknown sensations of pain and pleasure. Her mouth was now constantly open, and her breathing was of a staccato nature. Her fingers tightened as a reaction of caution as to what was to come; then a calmness as a gesture of acceptance while Mother Nature made allowance for the new 'arrival' who was about to enter, as yet, unopened accommodation.

I noticed a change in Brigitte's demeanour, as if enveloped by an ease of tension with the advent of her new-found (land) self, mixed with her precipitous excitement to try it out to experience new sensations! Her eyes closed as she threw her arms around my neck. "Thank you, Bernie."

"Satisfaction guaranteed, or your money back!" She released her grip around my neck and lay back on the bed. We lay in silence for a while. Then, of her own volition, she arched her back and raised her hips as a gesture of submission and temptation — and we were off again. Brigitte was now on a new sexual plane. As I penetrated her, even further (is there no end to this passageway?), she let out a groan from deep within her fibre — primeval in timbre. I pushed her and pulled her into numerous and varied positions. I had become animalistic and greedy for more and more — unchartered territory. She screamed, scratched and screeched, "Harder! Harder! Harder!" I was banging her for all I was worth, eventually 'Knocking on Heaven's Door!' But Brigitte had become insatiable; she couldn't stop, thrusting and jerking for more and more.

As a young stallion I had much spermatozoa in stock and felt its compelling momentum to burst free into the outside world, albeit, within the velvet constraints of Brigitte's 'pink tube!' I was about to ejaculate and evacuate the confines of paradise. I wanted to go out with a "big bang from the pink hole!" I leant forward and placed my lips on Brigitte's, whilst pinching her left nipple at the same time; pleasure and pain for some women is the ultimate sensation and Brigitte was up for it! I was still banging her as hard as I could. She was biting and scratching, her head swaying from side to side; our pelvic girdles crashing together. And then, 'cum and behold!' we culminated at the same time. I had successfully utilized 'coitus interruptus', albeit to Brigitte's chagrin. Long streaks of white were running off her belly from the pool in and around her belly button.

We lay there, savouring the moment.

Memories of My Way!
1961

Eventually Brigitte and I ventured outside into the cauldron of smoke, music and noise, just to be sociable. We soon became aware of an atmosphere of animosity towards us, from both sexes. We couldn't understand why; what had we done wrong? Brigitte and I had a couple of drinks but only had eyes for each other. Nobody spoke to us. Due to the animosity towards us, I smelt trouble but I followed the words of El Paso (Marty Robbins).

"But my love for Felina (Brigitte), was stronger than my fear of death."

So, this time, when we got back into the bedroom and closed the door, I pushed a large, heavy wardrobe along the floor until it was squarely in front of the door to thwart any potential intruders. Brigitte and I got straight into it. This time I lasted longer and Brigitte loudly vocalised her pleasure. This triggered the inevitable; there was knocking and banging on the door, then pushing the door against the wardrobe. Why would they want to do that? Jealousy! Jealousy of Brigitte and

I doing what they were THINKING of doing. It has become 'my cross to bear?' And still is — doing, what others think of, doing!

Brigitte and I got dressed quickly and waited 'til the noise had settled. I opened the door, not knowing what might happen. We boldly walked out amidst wolf whistles, cat calls and derogatory remarks and innuendos. We managed to get a taxi and I took Brigitte home. I saw her the next day, speeding along on the back of a silver 150cc Vespa scooter. Also, the next day, much to my chagrin, I discovered that some of my records had gone missing. I asked around but nobody knew anything. I also received more unfavourable innuendos. The main gripe was that I hadn't been out helping to pull birds for the party! But deep down I knew the real reason for their griping — they were jealous! Jealous because I had fucked the best of the bunch; then she went back to the bedroom with me for more!

The gang was becoming increasingly outrageous. They would steal from shops inside and stalls outside. John was going out at night, alone, to burgle chalets — MAD! I didn't want to be associated; furthermore, my money was running low. I had enjoyed myself to date but felt trouble looming. So, I decided to go back home, albeit after resisting the overtures of Brigitte's friend, who just wasn't in the same league. She made it quite clear that she wanted me to 'bed' her. I deduced that Brigitte had told her friend about her 'flight', which she had experienced with me, on that well-known Irish Airline (bed), AIR LINGUS (as in Cunni*****s!) and wanted the same turbulence. NO WAY!

Memories of My Way!
1961

Earlier in the year I had told Mum and Dad that I just hated working in an office in the City of London. I hated the commuting, be it via the crowded buses or tube (London Underground Trains). I hated the hustle and the bustle and the smoke from selfish 'fag' smokers, who at that time, could smoke anywhere! I hated the feeling of claustrophobia, being packed together in train carriages and buses like sardines. I could not identify with this mode of transport or lifestyle. I was used to getting around on my Dawes Double Blue, ten-geared bicycle, in a state of freedom! I was not into this commuting via public transport nonsense at all. I did try commuting by bike a few times from Hornsey Rise N19, to Leadenhall Street in the City but by the time I arrived at the office, I was either hot and sweaty or cold and wet from the rain; then I had to find somewhere to park my bike.

I also did not identify with working inside an office, I felt so claustrophobic. I was back — in prison! The work was also boring; it was tantamount to playing with bits of paper. No one advised me, managed me or directed me. Plus, the other employees were 'hoity-toity', pompous and snobbish, invariably from the southern Home Counties. Once again, I was a 'square peg in a round hole'.

So, what's new?

Although Dad had vowed that I would not get involved in the building trade (latterly known as the construction industry), he eventually proclaimed that, 'You had better come along with me'. That meant to join him on site; a building site. The site from who's hoarding he had jumped at the commencement of the year, 1961, to accompany me on the interview for the job, from which I was now about to escape. The thought of joining him on site, excited me.

Both sides of my family had been working in the building trade for generations. My father had been a bricklayer from leaving school; both my maternal and paternal grandfathers were bricklayers, also maternal and paternal uncles. My maternal uncle was now a contracts manager working with an old established building contractor out of Kingston-on-Thames, Surrey. My paternal uncle was a clerk of the works (also ordained), had culminated his career by becoming Clerk of the Works to the Royal Family, working out of Windsor Castle (decades before the fire, I might add). So, building was in my blood.

I recall Dad sitting me down and advising me of the harsh realities of the building trade. Cold winters, rough conditions, tough, crude men, that I would need to stick up for myself. So, what's new? Dad had long ago taught me how to look after myself, with bad intentions, and so had my maternal grandfather, who had been an amateur boxer and runner for Highgate Harriers. Furthermore, I had learned how to use my tongue from my mother and maternal grandmother. So, I was well equipped, ready willing and able!

In 1961 there was no such thing as thermal underwear/jackets. Men did not wear gloves or hard hats, they just became hardened to the hardships of the building trade. It was my time to become 'hard!' I was up for it! My body and soul were crying out to feel something — to do something — to achieve something! I wanted to use my boundless ENERGY in a constructive way. And yes, to begin with, I felt a lot of physical pain but I loved it! It was what I needed! I challenged myself on a daily basis to overcome — and overcome I did! Dad told me that I would need to study for City & Guilds in Brickwork. I enrolled at the North London Polytechnic in Holloway Road (not far from the new Arsenal Football Stadium), now known as North London University. I was excited; I was going to learn an historic and honourable trade.

As a quick aside, there was an English female comedian who said that Tony Blair's interpretation of further education was to put a few paintings in a bus shelter and call it a university!

As a further test of my resolve to join the building trade, Dad arranged for me to accompany him on a tour of the Cancer Research laboratories site in Lincoln's Inn Fields, Holborn, west of the City of London, one Saturday morning. The 'Fields' is actually a small square-shaped park in the central area of the Lincoln's Inn, which itself is a much larger square formed by magnificent and glorious Georgian architecturally-styled buildings. The square was originally built for the legal profession in the 1660s after the Plague and Great Fire of London and is still prominently so. The Old Curiosity Shop is close by, on the corner of a side street. The building of the laboratories was completed in 1962 — and there is STILL NO cure for cancer! What do they do in there — everyday? The finished construction is a monstrosity! It is a disgrace and an insult to the architects of yesteryear. It stands out for its urbanized mediocrity and non-aesthetic sensitivity. It is a crude red cube, sprawling over the ambiance emanating from the sophisticated historic structures and the sereneness of the park and its natural beauty.

So Dad took me around the site of the red cube (maybe Picasso contributed to the design); it was big with building materials everywhere. I had to watch my step otherwise I would have been, 'arse over tit!' The surroundings were rough and the men tough — but friendly.

"Morning 'Arry! This your boy?" (Actually, I was 17 at the time.) Greetings from one of the more genteel workers who also wore a shirt and tie, and the obligatory cloth cap, just like dad.

"Yeah! Showing him around the site; he wants to come into the building game." Dad answered.

Genteel Worker: "What the fuck does he wanna do that for? Mixing with all this shit. He looks like a bright boy to me."

Dad: "That's what I told him but you know what they're fucking like, these days. He wants to find out for himself."

Genteel Worker: "Yeah! You're fucking right there 'Arry! Best of luck, son. See you later 'Arry."

That was the first time I had ever heard my dad swear. It cut through me, like a knife through butter. Furthermore, I noticed a different demeanour about him. He had a swagger in his gait, more confident than at home. His voice was louder and altogether stronger, overall, in a spin of buoyancy. I soon came to realize that, in the building trade, there was sarcasm at best, f'ing and blindin' at most and fighting at worst. And, I came to learn that Dad had a streak of madness in his character, something of which I had not experienced before.

As Dad and I traversed further and further into the bowels of the three-basement building, the stench intensified. No toilets on building sites in those days. Don't ask the obvious; what do you think? The dark corridors were lit with occasional light bulbs, 'speared' into miles of overhead electrical cabling. It was like being in a smelly cave. Eventually we were back upstairs into natural light; no elevators. Dad took me over to where some bricklayers were building a wall. I was immediately mesmerized by their skill. It was like magic, watching individual bricks laid, at speed and precision. It required physical exertion, sharp eyes, delicate but firm touch, sensitivity to level and plumb (upright) plus a sense of urgency. I wanted that! I wanted to learn how to do that! I wanted the skill and aesthetic satisfaction. I wanted to be a bricklayer! I knew it was going to make me feel proud, worthy and revered.

Someone walks up to two bricklayers on a building site and says, "What are you doing?"

One bricklayer says, "I'm laying bricks."

The other bricklayer says, "I'm building a Cathedral!"

"What we need in life are more bricklayers and less architects!"

Memories of My Way!
1961

Most of all — I felt FREE!

By now it was August '61 and there I was, clocking-on at 7.45 am on my first day as a bricklayer improver (something I detested at Ernest F. Moy but here I loved it) on the Y.J. Lovell building site in Lincoln's Inn Fields, Holborn, London. I felt somewhat awkward in my hobnail boots, cluttering around together with my wearing far more clothing than necessary that Mum caringly insisted that I wore. The whole scenario was somewhat nerve wracking; it was different than anything I had previously experienced. It was new! Even at the tender age of seventeen I had already crossed several physical and psychological barriers (and there were lots more to come). I was confident, I just had to overcome my feelings of awkwardness, naivety and unworldliness. This was a world of MEN! Strong, rough, tough men. Men who were immensely durable, with a 'can-do' attitude — no hard hat protection then. There was no such thing as 'can't', or 'we'll do it tomorrow'. IT had to be done — now! 'We can get over that,' was the mentality and execution. Any notion of dissent was perceived as tantamount to bone idle, shirker, ponce. The perpetrator of which would be summarily ostracized. There were Men with strange sounding voices and accents, gaits and demeanours; I could not understand them to begin with, albeit they were from all over the British Isles. Men from various parts of England, Ireland, Scotland and Wales. My memories from this period of my working life are raw, real and revealing. Raw because all the experiences were without airs and graces, frills, humbug. Real because I was in a real world, with real men, in real situations. Revealing because I was on the verge of learning an historic and honourable trade. Moreover, I was on the precipice of learning more — about me!

The 'brickie' work force was large. Fifteen brickies plus four–six apprentices, 'toing & froing' Y.J Lovell Sites. Now here comes the 'rub'. Wally, the chain-smoking bricklayer foreman and seasoned building trade worker, managed to get me started as a bricklayer improver, i.e. 'making good', 'patching up' after bricklayers had finished working on various brickwork projects, at the princely sum of GBP 13.0s.0d, per week! This was in 1961 and twice what I was getting in that boring and claustrophobic office. And I later learned, more than the apprentices. Why? I never knew. However, it took me only six months to know more than all of them put together and burn them all off the line! (One at a time!) I was determined to validate, justify and deserve my wages and beat them all, at anything — knowledge, application and speed! And I DID!

This attitude was conceived and impregnated into my sub-conscious mind to believe and then achieve! A CAN DO and DO IT NOW attitude. This choice of attitude in my early life has held me in good stead over the years and still does! "Whatever the mind can conceive and believe it can achieve!"

In addition to studying for City & Guilds in Brickwork, I also enrolled, of my own volition, in an ICS international correspondence course in basic building, which gave an overview of the building trade. I subsequently bought a set of building books off a salesman who came onto a subsequent site on which I was working.

Dad also recommended another book, which specialized in all forms and applications of brickwork. Apparently, his brother Len, who retired as Clerk of the Works to the Royal Family, living in Windsor Castle, had gleaned much knowledge from the said book to enhance his progress within the building trade — so I bought that as well. I loved being in the building trade, especially brickwork. I was totally fascinated by it. Even 'Our Saviour', Winston Churchill, liked to lay a few bricks now and then.

"When I was a bricklayer, I laid bricks; then, as a young man, I laid chicks; now that I'm older — I just wanna get laid!"

Furthermore, my two main mentors also worked in the building trade; Jesus, a carpenter and Socrates, a mason. It engenders a philosophic faith!

Then, I got lucky! Lego bricks 'developed' onto the market place. Although, primarily for children, I could see the practical application of them for increased knowledge. The red bricks and white lintels were manufactured to scale with the real thing. I think the scale was one Lego brick to nine of a full-size brick inclusive of perceived bed-joints and cross-joints. There were also 'bats', half brick and closers, quarter bricks. This, for me, was so exciting because it opened up a whole new world of capability, at speed. It meant that I would know how to build any brick wall, irrespective of bond or thickness of wall and return, at the corner, into another bond. To me, this was a 'masterstroke' because historically, the setting out of brickwork, on site, had been done 'dry', by trial and error, with real bricks on the ground. This method was slow and laborious, but I could now do it, in seconds. I did not go as far as taking my little plastic bricks on site — that would have caused a stir but what I did do was to commit to memory the layouts of the various bonds and varying widths of walls. And then, Eureka! I found the 'secret' to brickwork bonding. As with all persistent endeavours, in truth, the answer WILL unfold. I say unfold because the truth is always, already there, it just needs to be discovered; like electricity.

The secret? No secret — the truth- the answer. The answer was already there, just waiting to be discovered, as the answer. The closer was the answer the quarter brick 2 ¼ inches wide. This is what creates the 2 ¼" bonding throughout the wall. It is the element of the wall, which creates the bond. A 'header' is then laid to the left of the closer. Since this revelation- I've been 'closing' ever since!

"What do you prefer, weekly or monthly?"

"Let's put a proposal forward to the underwriters!'

"Let's get this telephone answering machine installed, before you lose any more business!"

"What am I going to take off first? Your bra or panties?"

"OK! I'll take off your glasses first!"

My knowledge of brickwork went into overdrive including the 'springing points' to draw all and every arch that is imaginable; niches, buttresses, flying buttresses, circular ceilings, tunnels, footings, even the ingredients of the bricks themselves.

"Some chicks are similar to bricks; hard as nails — Staffordshire Blues; tough and rough — stocks; plain and simple — flettons; hot to trot — phosphorous firebricks; strong and uniform — semi-engineering (brick); showy — facing bricks; straight and upright- soldiers (bricks laid on their header ends). But the ones I like the most are the soft 'red rubbers' because they can be 'rubbed to perfection!'

Laying bricks is like laying chicks. First, prepare an ample bed; rub them securely in position, then squeeze the cross-joint, until extrusion. Picking up chicks is like picking up bricks; choose the ones that will lay easily.

Once chosen, bed them firmly, then iron in their joint(s) delicately!"

Memories of My Way! 1961

So, my time was full throughout the week, working five 1/2, sometimes six days each week and earning good money, even after the parasitical tax man had stolen his percentage. I LOVED my work! My evenings went like this

Monday: swotting for ICS course in Basic Building. Tuesday: City & Guilds Brickwork — theory. Wednesday: completing ICS assignment for that week. Thursday: C&G practical.

Friday: down to the Old School, Fortess Rd. NW5 to play table tennis with my mates, then across the road to have a few beers in the pub.

Saturday: drinking, dancing, wenching! Sunday: football, drinking, cinema.

I loved my lifestyle! I was growing — physically, mentally and emotionally. It was great!

The routine went on for more than a year. The upside being that I was learning a trade and enjoying my football and social life. The downside, that I was being ostracized at my place of work, due to my 'bastardised' position of bricklayer improver and advanced intellect. I was also somewhat lonely and sometimes embarrassed to be with my 'different' father. At home Dad was quite quiet but at work he could be verbal and dangerously manic! He would go into fits of rage resulting in bricks, mortar scaffold boards and bandstands flying all over the place. Nobody went near him when he flew into one of these rages. I learned that, years before, he had twice ruptured himself by picking up metal wheelbarrows and throwing them as far as he could. He was immensely strong, especially for his size. He was about 2" taller than me at 5'9" and about three quarters of my width. His muscle definition was honed out of sheer hard work and at forty-eight, in 1961, he was extremely fit and agile. His persona, on site, changed as did that of other workers. They were demonstrative and verbose, as though let out of a cage, albeit a domestic one! I felt similar, albeit free — free to burn up my phenomenal energy level, without anyone getting hurt. I could work just as hard as I wanted — and I did!

I remember working in dark, dank and smelly areas of the building, invariably in one of the three basements, carrying my electric light bulb with me, on my own, 'making good'. This was repair work and filling up holes which put me in good stead for my later addiction in life! It was dark, awe inspiring and lonely but my solace was ALWAYS with me — my singing, albeit under my breath. Most people smoked cigarettes — I sang songs to comfort me. In the navy, for the same reason, even in '61, sailors had to drink grog! Grog? Half a mug of rum and water. It became a tradition but initially it was a necessity, to ease the hardships of naval life. Napoleon's armies, "Marched on their bellies; Nelson's fleets, sailed on their bladders!"

Through the solace gained whilst singing and my new-found love of the building trade, I resolved that I would be The Best! I knew, in my water (rum), that I had an innate 'feel' for the building trade. It was rough, tough but also creative and aesthetically rewarding. My eyes grew sharp for level and 'plumb'. Plumb? Plumb Bob! Plumb Bob — what the pluck is that? Before spirit levels were designed, upright was determined by a wooden board, about three and a half inches wide and six feet long with a line cut into the middle of the board from top to bottom. At the top of the board there was a string attached, running down its length, with a stone shaped as a plumb attached to the end of the string, towards the bottom of the board. Three inches up, from the bottom of the board, would be a plumb-shaped hole, through which the stone would swing. When the narrow string swung, with movement from the board, initiated by the bricklayer. For the brickwork to be deemed upright/plumb, the string must fall into the crevice of the cut line, down the length of the board, perfectly! (Wow! I wish I had never started that!)

I had started on the Y.J. Lovell site in Lincoln's Inn Fields in August 1961 immediately after my holiday in Jaywick, Sands, Clacton-on-Sea, Essex, with all that happened there! Everything was strange on-site and after one week, also strange in me. I was experiencing an acute burning sensation whilst urinating. The inside of my penis was itchy and dried yellow puss appeared on my underpants. In my ignorance I concluded that this might be due to my new environment, albeit rough and dusty surroundings; maybe dust and cement had found its way into my dick. Furthermore, there were no urinals or wash hand basins. Maybe I had touched my dick with cement-covered fingers. The pain increased. I mustered the courage to tell my parents in the perceived belief that my new working environment was the culprit. I think Mum and Dad had other ideas and so I visited Dr Nathan, the 'family' doctor, whose surgery was in lower Sussex Way, across Tollington Way. Dr Nathan was a Jewess (well at least I was circumcised) who had known me all my life and recommended circumcision when I was two years of age. Ouch! Also ordering an ambulance on a Sunday afternoon, after diagnosing acute appendicitis about to burst and immediately operated on at the age of eight! After a short verbal and physical (my you've grown) investigation, she suspected STD.

Memories of My Way And the 60's!
1961

Sexually Transmitted Disease! Back then, in 1961, it was usually gonorrhoea or syphilis and to be honest I thought I was a goner, really! How? Who? Could only be, the beautiful and voluptuous, 'Brigitte', Belinda. I could not believe it. So beautiful! So clean! So soft. So plucking, pluckable. But of course, disease is on the inside and not the outside. Possibly did not know she had 'it' herself and only sixteen! But how? Clacton-on-Sea, geographically, is on the coast, the east coast of southern England. Ships would come in to Clacton, or nearby ports, with seamen, either coming home from some far-flung part of the world, or foreigners, flush with money, ready to pay for sex. It has only dawned on me, whilst writing this book, that Belinda, at age sixteen, was a freelance prostitute! That's why we never met again — I never paid her!

But the scenario now before me, after the 'fun and fireworks', was embarrassing. Not only embarrassing but downright shameful and frightening. Dr Nathan, the family doctor (a female of the Jewish persuasion who, when I was two years of age recommended that I be circumcised; then at age eight, ostensibly saved my life by quickly ordering an ambulance to rush me off to the Whittington Hospital at the Archway, to undergo an immediate operation to remove an appendix, which was about to burst; so much, for the ability to take pain!), instructed me to visit the Royal Northern Hospital in Holloway Road, ironically, where I had been born seventeen years earlier. I undertook a simple test which was diagnosed and confirmed, there and then. Yeah! I had gonorrhoea. When I told my parents, we all cried; I had never seen my dad cry before. I felt bad about myself. So bad that I told no one, until now. Why do so now? I do so now as a revelation for others to learn or laugh by, in their own way, as an endeavour to alleviate, anxiety, non-revelation and fear. Just get it sorted!

In 1961, just sixteen years after the end of WWII, hospital treatment was rudimentary. I will never forget the 'seasoned' doctor's method of extracting semen from my penis as evidence for diagnosis — he stuck his finger up my rectum, with great aplomb! (Obviously done it before, a few times) He rolled a red rubber glove onto his hand and applied a solution to his chosen finger. I was already standing with my legs astride, trousers and underpants around my ankles following the command, 'drop 'em!' I'm sure the doc was ex-military — forthright and confident. 'Been there, done that and seen every size and shape of dick imaginable; threw the pics away!' He was verbose and witty, keeping the surgery in fits of laughter with such comments as, "I remember your dick, but I've forgotten your face!" Albeit behind closed curtains. This choice of humour was, 'Just what the doctor ordered', to break the fear-riddled atmosphere.

At the time, I considered his method of extracting semen from my penis to be a neat trick but later, as I read more, I came to learn that the doc had found my G spot! For the record, no one has found it since! And there it was, just what he needed, to diagnose my problem. No point in fiddling around, worrying about which civil rights group he might upset, or which Tom, Dick, Harry and his dog 'movement' might be aggrieved. There it was, hot in the receptacle, for examination, before our very eyes!

OMG! Mummy! Penicillin injected into my posterior with a pneumatic drill! That's what a hypodermic needle seemed to look like and definitely felt like, in 1961. My thoughts flashed back to school when us kids, in the '50s had to queue in the assembly hall and wait our turn for torture to be administered on our young arms. And adding salt to the wound, also hearing the screams and seeing the gyrations of our school friends, as each endured their individual pain. It was called — 'immunisation'; all the rage in the '50s. Immunisation against, you name it. But I got lucky — Mum didn't believe in it; apart from poliomyelitis. Why was poliomyelitis acceptable for immunisation in her mind? I did a lot of swimming in pools, Highgate Ponds, rivers and the sea; stagnate water can be a cause of poliomyelitis, as far as she believed. Also, she went through WWII from age 23–29 and afterward, often referred to Franklin Delano

Roosevelt, the American President who, at the time, suffered from poliomyelitis. I recall, quite vividly, getting receiving in my arm, now I was going to get the same projectile in my bum! I'll never forget it, as long as I have a hole in my…

    I was standing facing the wall, as though I was about to be whipped. The injection of penicillin was to be administered by a female nurse. I was tense and muscular and so the nurse was having trouble inserting the needle. On the fourth attempt, I swear she threw it, like a dart; I felt it dangling! Then, I could feel the penicillin exploding into my bloodstream and my right leg simultaneously stiffening and weakening. It went on and on; I felt weak, faint and humbled. I struggled to bend down and pull up my pants and trousers. But! She was worth it!

Memories of My Way!
1961

The next few weeks were traumatic, at home, work and socially. At home the atmosphere was tense; at work I was having to leave late afternoon, twice a week to receive my treatment at the Royal Northern Hospital situated in Holloway Road, from the site in Holborn, West Central London. (This also did not gel well with the apprentices — new boy on the block, going home early. If only they knew why.) And in retrospect, it has only just recently dawned on me that Wally, the bricklayer foreman must have known (via Dad), because he never queried my motives for leaving early. I was also off the booze (on doctor's orders), much to the curiosity of my friends because, even at seventeen, I did like a pint (at two bob a pint!) or two and therefore strange, not to see me drinking. Anyway, I just did what I always do — I kept on, 'keeping on!' After a month, I was cured! Thank God!

However, that scenario, plus the scare with Gina, just over a year previously, put me off girls for a couple of years. I'd had sex with only two girls and on both occasions, found myself in trouble.

So, I poured my energy into my work and football. The team was a fusion of Old Boys from Acland Central Boys and Burghley Road Schools, close to each other in Tufnell Park, London, NW5. But inexplicably, the fusion formed a gel, which created a winning team. So much so that at the end of the 1961/62 season we had won three trophies (typically playing at Regent's Park NW5 and Hackney Marshes E8)! We won two 'knock-out' cups plus coming top of the division in the Regent's Boy's League (boys meant to be under twenty-one).

Then to cap it all, our trophies were presented to us by 'big head' himself. No, not Brian Clough but Leslie Compton, the previous centre half for Arsenal Football Club and the England Football Team; also playing first class cricket for the MCC — Middlesex Cricket Club, just like his brother Denis, of Brylcreem renown!

So here comes the Acland-Burghley Old Boys Football Team.

Goalkeeper: Dennis McKee. Strong, brave, creative. Right back: Brian Reynoldson. Tenacious, wiry, fast.
Left back: Tony Goodyear. Immaculate, efficient, creative
Right half: Bernard Tetlow. Strong tackler, creative, goal scorer.
Centre half: Johnny Saunders. Strong, brave, awkward.
Left half: Colin Croggon. Determined, experienced, vision.
Outside right: Barry Orton. Fancy, good crosser, poacher.
Inside right: Andy Choralambous. Ball control, creative, resilient. Centre forward: Andy Adams. Strong, fast, opportunist.
Inside left: Costa Adams. Control, hard, accurate kicker.
Outside left: Reggie Bacchus. Right place, right time, poacher.

	Acland Burghley 1961-62 2 Cups & League	Spurs 1961-1962 1st Double Winners of 20th Century	England 1966 World Cup Winners
Goalkeeper (Burghley)	Dennis McKee	Bill Brown	Gordon Banks (Leicester)
Right back (Acland)	Brian Reynoldson	George Cohen	George Cohen (Spurs)
Left back (Acland)	Tony Goodyear	Henry/Baker	Ray Wilson (Everton)
Right half (Acland)	Bernie Tetlow	Dave Mckay	Nobby Stiles (Man. Utd.)
Centre half (Burghley)	Johnny Saunders	Maurice Norman	Jack Charlton (Leeds)
Left half (Acland)	Colin Croggon	Danny Blanchflower	Bobby Moore (West Ham)
Outside-right (Acland)	Barry Orton	Terry Dyson	Alan Ball (Arsenal)
Inside right (Acland)	Andy Charalambous	Jimmy Greaves	Geoff Hurst (West Ham)
Centre forward (Burghley)	Andy Adams	Bobby Smith	Bobby Charlton (Man. Utd.)
Inside left (Burghley)	Costa Adams	John White	Roger Hunt (Liverpool)
Outside left (Acland)	Reggie Bacchus	Cliff Morgan	Martin Peters (West Ham)

Memories of My Way
And the 60s!

The football season moved towards Christmas, of which I remember little; in fact, nothing!

I am not attracted to the superficiality of the premeditated, orchestrated and perceived happiness of Christmas and all that it is meant to represent and uphold. I personally, do not need to be given license to enjoy myself; I do it all of the time!

Christmas is a 'gravy train' for shops, supermarkets, and all and sundry who sell something! And invariably owned by members of another religious persuasion that persecuted the originator of Christmas. The whole affair is hypocritical and contradictory — and, of course a manipulation of the flock syndrome. New Year is the same, if not more so. People of varying denominations performing totally out of character gesticulations and antics, as some kind of expression of contrived exuberance due to the approach of a contrived new year. It appears to me, to be an enormous release of pent-up frustrations, amassed during the previous year of, in short, non-fulfilment. Non-fulfilment of numerous degrees; basically of not doing what the participants would really, rather have done but did not have the courage to try. A release of regret! However, my maxim is — 'Do It NOW!' And then, when one does do it now, positive chemicals are released into the brain which, I believe, attract positive reaction. Proactive not reactive. 'Accentuate the positive, eliminate the negative!'

'The quickest way to learn, is to put your nuts on the line!' (anBw). "Fear is the best motivator!"

I hate humbug! From a kid I could not take humbug! I recall, on one particular occasion in the mid-1950s, Mum, Dad and I, being invited by my Aunt Maude to Lyon's Corner/Coffee Shop in Piccadilly Circus. As far as I remember, it was a glorified, 'buffet' coffee shop, albeit popular around London, with a branch actually being located at the Archway, near to where I was living at the time. Maude was, in fact, Mum's Father's younger sister, in effect Mum's aunt but of a similar age. My maternal great-grandfather, produced seven children; Bill, George (my grandfather), Arthur, Wally, Lillian, Eddie and Maude. Maude produced four; John, Michael, Hilary and Janet. It was Michael who spoke for me in 1963 and arranged the interview as an insurance agent, which introduced me to sales! And, just for the record, Lillian was the mother of Anthony Newlands, (not Newley) who became a regular actor on the TV. He had a regular part as a judge in a long-running series on one of the TV channels.

Anyway she, Maude, was a Snob, with a capital 'S'. Albeit dragged up from the gutters of Hornsey Rise, North London — like me. But by the time I came along, the gutters weren't quite so dirty. She worked her husband (of Irish extract) to the bone. He was a carpenter but with a difference; he worked on TV and film sets and earned good money, working weekends an' all! "Working all the hours God sends!" was a favourite remark of Mum.

They had a car! And for working class folk in the mid-50s, that *WAS* something else! And, I've got to give them credit, they also toured Europe. WOW!

"We've just come back from the Conthonont! Oh, the south of France is SO beautiful!"

I recall their car being covered in GB badges.

So, here we all are, on a Sunday afternoon, the summer of '55/'56, at Lyons Corner House, Piccadilly; my Mum, Dad, Arthur and Maudie. Oh my God! Aunt Maud's accent changes immediately — she's trying to talk posh! I'm looking at her and wondering why she wants to sound so stupid. She's only talking to a waiter for pluck's sake; probably out of East London, who has heard all this humbug, before — ten thousand times. Then Mum joins her and chimes in with, "What would you like, Hhhh-Harry?" My dad is like 'torn between the devil and the deep blue sea'. My dad was no snob but had a sensitivity for people's feelings, "Cup of tea 'll do me!" I could see he, like me, wanted out, but how, without appearing rude.

We were all done up to the nines — smart. I felt extremely uncomfortable and socially claustrophobic. I hated it! I hated wearing my jacket, long trousers, shirt and tie, especially at age twelve. Who were we trying to please? The whole episode was a complete façade. It left an indelibly revengeful impression on my sub-conscious mind. So much so that when I have and do, feel that enveloping environment of conformity, I rebel. I WILL be, outrageous, verbally and physically. I will NOT conform to pomp and ceremony, to atmospheres contrived by some, to extract servitude, manipulation and control!

Memories of My Way!
1961

There have been occasions, over the years, where I have exercised my contempt for contrived entrapment in respect of over-the-top etiquette. Two come to mind, both in the 90s, I believe; both in London.

1) I was having dinner, not lunch (dinner is the main meal of the day, irrespective of time), with a few insurance sales colleagues at a plush restaurant in Mayfair in the West End of London, one of the richest areas of the world. We had been invited there by the branch manager (who was the brother of Bruce Rioch), of Royal Life's Piccadilly branch, ironically, just around the corner from Lyons Corner House of forty years earlier. So, I'm looking through the menu but it's all written in French! I don't speak French and therefore don't read French, albeit my family name is a derivation of Tete-de-Loup! (See what I mean; figure it out for yourself). And, believe it or not, I was pretty good in French whilst at school, but I was not in school now — I was in a restaurant and I was not in France, I was in London — and I was there to eat food, not to have a

lesson in French!

So, all the other fellas have their heads buried in their menu, hoping, nay praying, that somebody will say something about their possible choice of meal so they can say, "Yes! I was thinking of having that myself!" Not knowing what the pluck it was anyway. The silence was deafening and got louder and louder; from the start I was outraged by this pseudo-entrapment game to exude more money from unsuspecting customers, due to their ignorance and embarrassment but I thought, keep cool Bernard. However, by now the cooling system was on the point of boiling!

"Excuse me! Why is the menu written in French? I am an Englishman in England; I can't read or speak French. I come here to eat, not learn French!" I knew what was about to come out of this snob waiter's mouth would be condescending. I waited to determine the timbre of his voice and as soon as I heard it I cut across him with a broad nasal London accent.

"Lisen! Eever you git us Menoos in English, or, you tell us EVERYFING, in English, word-f'-word! Got it?" We got menus, written in English.

2) Not such a plush restaurant this time but still perceived as an up-market expensive area of North London — Winchmore Hill. It was somewhat an evening of reunion with four couples. The evening went well with much frivolity and laughter; eating and drinking. I recall the waiter being something of a schmuck/snob. He was occasionally passing condescending remarks and wanted us out for the next lot in! However, we were not ordering bottles of water; we were spending a few 'bob'.

Eventually, it was time to go. I asked for the bill and it came soon enough. I decided to be mischievous and contrived the bill to be some kind of delicacy as a gesture of goodwill, on-the-house, from the restaurant.

"Ah, thank you!" says I, and proceeded to push the bill into my mouth and chew on it! After a few seconds of astonishment, everyone burst into laughter, except the waiter — he had to write on the bill, again! He still got a good tip.

I hate pomp and ceremony, protocol and ostentation!

I love, discipline and organization, respect and transparency! Don't you?

Some of you might ask, "But Bernard, where was your discipline and respect in the above scenario?" And my answer would be this; it has taken me so many years to realize that when someone is an arsehole to you, they, inadvertently, give you license, to be an arsehole to them!

"You can't win a fight clean, if your adversary is fighting dirty!"

Memories of My Way!
1962

Off to work on 1st January 1962! Back then there was no national holiday on the first day of the year. It took character to get out of bed and get to work by 8.00 am on a cold, bleak and windy January morning, after partying to the early hours — but people did it!

By working conscientiously with my studies, I was learning at a prolific rate. So much so that the 'theory' City & Guilds tutor, who full time was a general foreman for Fairweather's, an old established and reputable building company, offered me a job! What? I'm only seventeen years of age, in the building trade for six months and I'm being offered a job. And not only that, I got my dad a job as a bricklayer foreman, to boot!

The site was in Berner's Street, off Oxford Street, in the West End of London; I think the project was to build shops and offices above. Dad and I started in February 1962. I remember Wally's face, the chain-smoking brickie foreman at the Cancer Research laboratories, where I had been working since August 1961, when I told him I was leaving. I think he was hurt, embarrassed and annoyed to think that this little me upstart had the gall to 'up tools' and go, after he had given me the opportunity to get into the building trade. In retrospect he may also have got some piss-taking from all and sundry on site. However, I never let him down, I worked hard and conscientiously.

Dad and I jogged along for a few weeks at Berner's Street but I could see that Dad was not comfortable with his role and responsibilities as a bricklayer foreman. Dad was a responsible person but did not like responsibilities. Personally, I was quite happy, albeit the site was much smaller than the Cancer Research laboratory and with less variety — but I was earning more money — and so was Dad!

Football was going great, winning virtually all of our matches; we had a great comradeship in the team. I was playing at right half back and relishing the sensation of crunching tackles, winning the ball and then laying off 'through balls' to inch perfect precision 'to feet!' ("I used to be modest but I couldn't see the point of it!"). I WAS Dave McKay of Spurs. I didn't care about how good you were, big you were or anything else, "YOU, are going up in the air!" But of course — ball first! Me and Davie Boy would be off the pitch after the first tackle, perhaps even before that, in the virtual non-contact sport that football has become, in the 21st century.

The 'Wind Beneath the Wings' of the team was Vic Corby, a bachelor and an old, Old, Old Boy of Acland Boy's School. He was the MD and owner of a heating and ventilating company in Farringdon Street, east of the City of London. In addition to organizing everything appertaining to our footballing fixtures, he additionally took, which at the time in 1962 was an enlightened decision, to have us boys/young men of age seventeen play football in Belgium and Holland during the forthcoming Easter Holy-days! Virtually unprecedented! My first trip abroad, from the shores of England, at age just seventeen on the 5th April; in 1962 — this was 'something else!' To play football — well that WAS exceptional! Ironically, this very same Easter, in Spa, Belgium, was to see one of my all-time sports characters on his virtual death-bed — Stirling Moss, English Formula 1 racing driver. Thank God he survived his near fatal crash and recovered, but never raced again.

Going abroad to play football! What a thrill! We travelled via train, could have been Waterloo to, I think it was Folkstone and then on to Ostend, by ferry. I can still sense the intense smell of diesel fumes, even to today, nauseating! The ship was quite basic, and I recall the recoil from the strong North Atlantic Ocean waves causing a whirling and swirling sensation in my stomach. It was in a state of turmoil and on the verge of catapulting its contents, up to and out of, my mouth! Most of the team were eating and drinking but not me. I am a more than competent swimmer but I can't take, to this day, being on a smallish vessel whirling around in the sea. I recall quite a number of years ago being in Puerto Buenos, before it become commercialised, diving off a small boat to swim to shore a few hundred yards distant, rather than continuing to heave my heart up.

Memories of My Way!
1962

As I recall, Ostend, Belgium, in 1962 was a quaint coastal town, we all stayed in large guest house with cobblestone streets and shop. I recall a profusion of exotic liqueurs, Cherry Brandy, Apricot Brandy, Pear Brandy, spoilt for choice. In my mind's eye, I can see Reggie Bachus with a bottle of 'something' stuck in his mouth; drinking beyond his capacity. The football matches, one in Belgium and one in Holland, were a blur but I think we lost both of them. I have nostalgic memories of the beer halls where large ladies would carry three to five litre jugs of beer to tables — in each hand! But the memories most predominant in my mind were of buying a variety of items for resale back in the UK. Many of the fellas on the Berner's Street site had ordered a multitude of items of which I was unaware were available in the 'low countries'. Cigars, watches, rings, bracelets, necklaces, ear-rings, cufflinks, tie pins. When I returned to the site and sold my gear, I had more than doubled my overall expenditure for the Easter trip. However, on opening my tool bag, I could not find my 10" Tyzak brick trowel. When Dad found out, he flew into a rage. He was virtually offering anybody out and challenging the unknown culprit to step forward. Dad was born in Dalston, London E9, but grew up in Finsbury Park; not far from Campbell Bunk! Within a month, Dad and I were off the site. We crept back to Y.T. Lovell at a site near Roseberry Avenue, near to Sadler's Wells Theatre. It was a block of flats, boring and repetitious. Thus commenced another influential period of my life. My Uncle Fred, my mother's younger brother, had progressed in the building trade from a bricklayer to foreman to general foreman and now contract's manager for a smallish building company by the name of GAZES, working out of Kingston-on-Thames, he had recently been appointed contracts manager to build a new police cadet college in Sunbury-on-Thames, 26 miles south-west of Hornsey Rise, London N19, where I was living. The site was currently in its early stages of clearance, whereby trees had to be felled and dwellings demolished. It was agreed for me to start after my summer holidays of '62. I was so excited.

The summer holidays of '62 saw my three close friends, Colin Croggon, Brian Reynoldson and Barry Orton at Butlin's, Holiday Camp in Bognor Regis, Butlin's being the 'brain-child' of (Sir) Billy Butlin, a working-class entrepreneur who saw massive opportunity to supply members of the opposite sex with an organized and legitimate facility for getting laid; especially the young working class. I recall meeting attractive and sexy girls with great 'huggable' bodies but as soon as they opened their mouths thick, unusual, accents would send my ear-drums and mind into a state of confusion and apprehension of persuading them to do anything else. I had a couple of encounters but not as far as to open any other orifice. I was still reelin' but not rockin' from my sexual experiences of '60 and '61! However, there are two incidents, clear in my mind, from that holiday.

From ages seven to fourteen I had done a lot of swimming. I had been awarded the Bronze Medallion at age fourteen for Life Saving. Also, third in breaststroke, London School Boys' Championships at age thirteen. I especially liked swimming underwater (away from the noise and maddening crowd), and could do that for the length of the fifty-yard pool. I remember the amazement on my maternal grandfather's face, when at age ten, I would dive into ten feet of water at the Finchley Outdoor Swimming Pool, and retrieve old pennies, halfpennies and farthings from the bottom; even a silver sixpence — no goggles! Subsequently, my shoulders and chest had filled-out to accommodate such activities.

So here I was, 'Jack the Lad', at eighteen, approaching the Butlin's pool, for the first time. Traditionally, diving boards are at either end of the pool but with this pool, they were in the middle, facing me, on the other side. I quickly deduced that the deep end must be in the middle of the pool. Due to my impatience to show-off, I nonchalantly turned around on the edge of the pool and did a back-flip dive. Ouch! Simultaneously the heels of my hand hit the bottom of the pool, then my elbows then my nose! I had dived into two feet of water! Fortunately, I was okay, my hands and elbows taking most of the impact; my nose has always been malleable.

Next! Colin advised me there was a swimming

competition to be held, so I entered for the breaststroke and guess what? Right! I won it! I was particularly chuffed because two or three days earlier I was advised by a physiotherapist at the good old Royal Northern Hospital to give my ankle complete and thorough rest which I had badly twisted larking about on the hillside leading down to the ponds at Parliament Hill. So, whilst winning the swimming competition, my ankle was heavily bandaged.

I was especially chuffed!

Then, the four of us, Colin, Brian, Barry and myself entered a five-a-side competition (we picked up a goalie from somewhere) and won it!

Memories of My Way!
May 1962

However, before those summer holidays there was more football to play. Our manager, Vic Corby, had entered us in two cup competitions; we had already won our division in the league, which meant one medal already in the bag. One down, two to go! We then played our first cup final at Regent's Park in North West London — and won! Two down, one to go!

Now we were to play our second cup final at Hackney Marshes in East London (where part of the 2012 Olympics was held), to make it three out of three. This was to be a much tougher match facing a team from a tougher league. And, to prove the point, we were 2-0 down at half time! At the break I recall saying something like, "I didn't come here to lose. I want that third medal!" I may also have lambasted a couple of players for not trying hard enough. I was the official free-kick taker for the team plus the throw-in taker on the right. My position was right half, number 4. We came out for the second half and I was demented to win! I vowed to myself that I would win every ball that I went for — and I did. And when I got the ball, it would go forward, every time. Then something amazing happened. I found that when taking throw-ins, the ball was travelling 30-50% further than usual! Due to my demented will to win, during the game I had inadvertently developed a new technique and power to throw the ball much, much further; it was almost as good as a free kick. It was surreal and caught the opposition on the hop. So much so that we scored two goals directly from my extended throw-ins. Then, unbelievably, we scored a third! We eventually won the match 3-2 and I would like to think that my performance, on the day and bizarre sequence of throw-ins, were contributory factors to the result. Even Corby congratulated me after the match, an unusual occurrence for me. The downside was that my triceps were 'killing me'.

So, we now had three trophies to collect and presentation day was looming. I decided to make a difference, by being different, albeit totally in keeping with the occasion. I ordered a new tailor-made double-breasted black blazer to be made, plus grey flannel trousers to match. Then the crowning glory — I 'acquired' an original Acland Boys School badge in yellow and black, plus yellow and black tie, pinned by a tie pin, which I bought whilst in Belgium. Was I the 'dog's bollocks', or what? Mum had stitched the badge onto my top jacket pocket, just as she had done when I first joined Acland Boys School, London NW5, in September 1955. I felt so proud when I stepped up, on three occasions, to receive my medals. Guess who was doing the presentation? Big Head! The affectionate name given to Leslie Compton, Arsenal's and England's centre half in the 50s. I have a picture of him gazing at me with admiration in his eyes as I passed after receiving one of my medals from him. He subsequently took the Prince of Wales pub in Highgate Village, London N6 but unfortunately, became riddled with arthritis.

The team, plus friends and relatives, celebrated afterwards on the first floor of the pub us lads frequented every Friday night, bang opposite our beloved school. I recall we presented Corby with a glass cabinet.

Memories of My Way!
1962

In the summer in '62 my Uncle Fred drove an orange minivan with the name GAZES (the building company he worked for) painted in black on either side. And here he comes, at 6.30 am on a Monday in early July 1962, driving along Hornsey Rise shopping parade, London N19. He is here to pick me up for my first day, on his new contract building site at Sunbury-on-Thames, Middlesex, twenty-six miles away. The project is a new police cadet college. I am a bricklayer improver; too old for an apprenticeship but too young to be a fully-fledged bricklayer. An oddity, from the start — and ever since!

Sitting next to Fred is Jack, of the old, old building trade school. He is a 'ganger man', the leader of ground workers in the building trade. His face is that of a British bulldog, with an aroma to match — albeit ruddy and weather-beaten from years of inclement weather toiling on building sites. He wore the obligatory cloth cap, the peak of which had, for years, shaded his forehead causing it to shine like a cumulus white cloud above the blazing sun of his face. He also sported the obligatory red and white spotted kerchief to cover his revealed neck caused by the also obligatory collarless shirt, associated with the hooligan image of the 30s and 40s but still of psychological influence in the early 60s. Next came the tight waistcoat with gold watch-pocket to boot, beneath an old suit jacket; enter — smart hooligan. His trousers were of a dark flannel style, shining with wear and grime. Jack is single and always has been, looking after himself. Every night he would be in his local pub sinking five, six, seven plus pints of beer and then sharing the contents in vapour form the next day, on site and unfortunately sometimes in the van. This would bring an immediate spray of expletives and sarcasm (of which he was a master) from my Uncle Fred, causing Jack acute embarrassment!

Jack was a character, especially on site; he was hardy and strong, sometimes showing, by example, his animalistic leadership qualities with exhibitions of his immense strength. He probably had no or little education, but what he did possess was an innate 'feel' and awareness of the building trade 'etiquette' and for building trade workers' attitudes. He epitomised the 'bully' but knew how to cause men to work. He had a big voice, big head, thick neck, big hands, big chest and could easily instil apprehension/fear into site workers with his awesome demeanour, aggressive body-language and his calculated, "f'ing and blindin'" — even at 5'9". NOBODY argued with him!

Uncle Fred could also 'put it about' at around 5'7". He was a master of sarcasm and could reduce big men to extreme embarrassment without retaliation due a base of truth of his observations, knowledge and words in respect of the individual's poor work ethic. He was my mother's brother and the pride and joy of her mother, my grandmother; much to my mother's psychological detriment. She was nine when Fred arrived and became bereft of her parents' attention due to the newborn infant. He somewhat resembled the facial features of Elvis Presley and possessed a fine tenor voice. In contrast to Jack, Fred wore a respectable suit and tie and played the part of his position as Contract Manager for GAZES. I admired him. "Working class boy, dun good!"

At 7.30 am we arrived on site. It was on a narrow, one-way street, so Fred took the left-hand fork of the Y junction and drove down to the T junction to turn right onto the Sunbury Road. As we approached the road, the River Thames crystallized into my eyesight; it was a pretty and picturesque view of the water, serene and tranquil with the early morning sun glistening on the surface, the green grass twinkling from the early morning dew.

Memories of My Way!

In the remaining winter of 62–63 nature caused the Thames to become an amazing spectacle, turning the top foot or so of water, from the surface, into ice!

Fred then turned right onto the Sunbury Road and another quick right with the Flower Pot Pub, on the corner — soon to be the Friday lunchtime local for some of us, especially the shuttering carpenters, one of whom virtually cut off one of his fingers when returning to the site after guzzling a few pints of beer in the designated lunchbreak time of half an hour!

As we turned right, on the left-hand side was a high 13 and 1/2" inch thick wall, no doubt to obtain privacy by the previous owners when originally built 200 plus years earlier. (Hampton Court is not far along the Thames, to the East.) I could see that it had been built in English garden wall bond and was now serving as the boundary wall for the building site. A few yards further along and there was the opening to drive onto the site. This building site would prove to be the setting, the stage, the springboard for my physical, mental and emotional growth. I was eighteen years and three months of age.

Memories of My Way!
1962

I am now in the house of pseudo-colonial style amongst a myriad of hardened and seasoned building trade workers, alone! Fred is in his office and Jack is nowhere to be seen. The vast majority of the men around me were tantamount to country yokels; twenty-six miles from London in 1962, was countryside. They are wary of me because I am a potential threat to their peace of mind and equilibrium. Number one, I am a 'city-slicker' from 'the smoke!' Number two, I am the nephew of 'The Boss!' Number three, my function on site was difficult for them to determine. I did not present them with a comfort zone of acceptance; I was indefinable, an enigma. Always was — always will be!

Soon I was out on site, doing what I loved, laying bricks; I began to relax.

Ten am was suddenly upon us and it was time to eat. The problem was that cuisine was back in the house, amongst the muck and gore. I got to sitting and eating outside the house to inhale fresh air. This kinda got to exacerbate my perceived oddity and created an image of aloofness on my part. I was not! I just wanted fresh air and to release my feelings of claustrophobia, which were enveloping my want and need, to be an individual, whilst inside the house.

It was early stages on site. Oversite concrete level had not yet been reached, this meant a lotta, lotta bricks had to be laid in the footings, to get to that level. JCBs had already been employed to dig down to the required depth of about six feet below ground level on the north side of the site and then footings being built, in places, six feet above the G/L, on the south side of the site. So, as you can imagine, the ground was sloping down, quite naturally and gracefully, to the River Thames. I spent a lot of time, a few weeks, working in the trenches, which were the width of a JCB 'shovel', about three feet wide, if that, pulling bricks from above me, stacked at ground level. And — I loved it!

After two or three weeks, three wooden huts were erected to accommodate us workers to eat; the aroma of clothes changing, etc. was, at last, 'blowing in the wind!'

Memories of My Way!
1962

Fred appointed another Jack to be bricklayer foreman. He was in his fifties and we struck up a friendship as building trade colleagues. I was fascinated by his refined style of laying bricks. He, himself, was also refined in that he always wore a clean shirt and tie to work, plus of course, the obligatory cloth cap and dungarees; just as Dad did, by the way.

Jack was an addicted conversationalist, and chain smoker but he knew his trade. His conversation was philosophical and enlightening. He was the person who taught me the phrase,

"Always question what appears to be the obvious."

The building trade at that time attracted, not exactly dropouts but more, non-conformists. Men who basically wanted to be individuals and free. Free from protocol, free from onerous rules and regulations — and The Establishment! I identified with these feelings. The trade attracted men who had a restless disposition, they wanted to move on — and they could — and they did, just apply at the next building site up the road, or anywhere, in the world!

Jack and I worked together. In retrospect I think Fred may have asked him to take me under his wing to teach me more of the refinements of bricklaying. So much so that after only five or six weeks of working at Sunbury, Jack and I were working on a chimney stack from ground floor level; the footings were already in. The stack was to eventually rise above the roof level of the three-storey college. The structure of the stack was unusual and the construction, challenging. The inner wall was of phenoseal bricks. These are very light to handle, fireproof bricks. The 'bed' is spread along the length of the brick with a brick trowel, just like spreading butter. Problems in level quickly arise if the bricks are not laid precisely. The phonoseals were laid to create an internal two-inch square, to form the size of the flue. Then flettons, common bricks, were laid adjacent to and around the phonoseals. These were followed by course of Crowborough facing bricks laid around the flettons. Crowboroughs were used to face the whole of the college. The plan view would show a two-inch flue with three varying types of brick. On each of the corners was built a 13.5" square, in facework. This meant that there were forty plumbing points, externally plus eight internally, to each course, plus the need to maintain a level equilibrium across three varying depths and types of brick; lot of spirit bubble work. Tedious but challenging — and I was loving it! And my life!

After two or three weeks, three wooden huts were erected to accommodate us workers to dine, twice a day; also porta-loos, which I never used, once — the stench, even on approach — was unbearable. I controlled myself!

The erection of the huts signalled the demolition and

demise of the 'old house'. I was about to be aware and experience my first aesthetic feelings for architecture and pride for heritage and history. As I watched the initial demolition, I tried to imagine what the life and times were like when 'she', the old house, was first built in what I deduced to be, the 1700s. It had been constructed in the Georgian era and of pseudo-colonial style, overly white in colour. It seemed to be such a waste and shame to pull it down — but down it came when the bulldozers marched in. I was choked, and a tear filled my eye.

There was talk at home between my mum and dad about buying a car. I was earning good money and could easily buy a scooter, either a Lambretta 175cc or a Vespa 150cc, preferably the latter. However, my mum, at fifty something was adamant that I was NOT going to have one; even though I was the one to pay for it. Why? Number one, as a kid and beyond, I had been in and out of hospital with a variety of injuries; I liked, nay loved, pushing the limits. She was convinced that I would kill myself on the back of anything motorised. I had already been off my pushbike many times previously receiving cuts, abrasions and bruises. However, on my Jacko Skates I had broken my right wrist; also, numerous, badly twisted ankles, facial cuts and bruises, dislocated finger, bloodied nose, chaffed gums, the list went on — and there was more to come.

In addition, my dad had been a keen motorbike enthusiast in the 30s. He had owned seven or eight bikes and belonged to a biking club around Turnpike Lane, London N8. If you drive a 41 bus from Turnpike Lane to Crouch End you will pass

Hornsey Train Station on the left. I recall, as a kid, in the mid late 50s, peering out of the bus window as we passed the station and seeing several small single-seater racing cars in the station sidings. Guess what? That's where Colin Chapman started Lotus!

During the mid-30s Mum and Dad, plus other members of the biking club must have created a precedent in that they organized a trip to ride their motorbikes, all the way to — Cornwall. And then to… stay in tents! What debauchery, I ask you! I think the occasion was repeated for two or three summers. However, on the last occasion, when Mum and Dad were riding back to London on the Guildford by-pass (where Mike Hawthorn was killed in 1958), Dad lost the bike on a corner dusted with gravel! They were both thrown off the bike and concussed (no helmets in those days), and rushed to hospital. Mum had facial cuts, especially above the left of her top lip; Dad had a deep scar on his head causing severe concussion. Dad never rode again. So, Mum was utterly adamant. No motorbike or scooter for Bernie Boy! We bought a car instead!

Memories of My Way! Summer of '62.

So, Mum, Dad and I went hunting for an appropriate car. The three of us took a 210, single-decker bus to Highgate Village where, during the week, Mum was 'charring'. There was, at that time, a car showroom on the corner of Highgate Village and the Spaniards Lane leading to the Spaniards Inn (of Dick Turpin repute) past the Bishops Avenue (millionaires row) on to Jack Straw's Castle at Hampstead Heath and then the Whitestone Pond (where I first learned to swim, without a life belt), down the hill to Hampstead Village.

Fortunately, Dad took a liking to an original Ford Escort which was an estate car (hatchback) based on the 1950s Ford Prefect/ Popular saloon cars. It was pale blue, 1100cc with three forward gears. When Mum was ready, she could be an extremely persuasive and determined lady; she sold Dad on buying the car there and then! It was August 1962.

Mum's motivation was not out of being desirous of owning a car but to keep me off the back of a scooter/ motorbike. When I had previously told her that I was going to buy a scooter she went into a panic of FEAR! I had a history of accidents with anything and everything in which I participated; in and out of hospital for most of my life.

"You'll kill yourself!" Mum screamed. "You'll go too fast and kill yourself, just like Johnny Rudge. You're a scatterbrain, just like him!" Johnny Rudge was a flamboyant character motorcyclist colleague/ friend of Mum and Dads who did ride his bike fast. I remember, on one occasion, he was speeding down Fairbridge Road, N19 (no traffic/parked cars then), waving to people as he flashed by, and yes, he did, eventually die as the consequence of a crash on his motorbike. Mum saw me as a second Johnny Rudge.

So, the Escort was summarily purchased, albeit on the 'never-never!' GBP 385. Dad put down GBP 200 deposit and I paid the rest on the HP. That's how I got to know how to get settlement figures from HP companies (with a small discount) via a red public telephone box! At age nineteen! The car and driving changed my life and made me restless for the next forty-five years!

Earlier in the year, during spring, after my eighteenth birthday, Uncle Fred had tried to teach me to drive in the minivan around the back streets of Seven Sisters Road as it approaches Tottenham Hale, but I couldn't get the hang of it. I followed his instructions precisely but the van kept stalling. He was telling me to depress the clutch to the floor, select first gear, then slowly raise the clutch and slowly depress the gas pedal. However, if he heard the gas before the clutch was fully extended, he didn't like it. The result was the clutch became fully extended with no gas, so the engine stalled. He stopped teaching me. And in retrospect it is ironic that exactly three years later I would pass my Advanced Driving Test at age twenty-one and became the youngest driving instructor for the British School of Motoring!

Memories of My Way!

So now we had a car but with no one to drive it! Ironically though, Dad did have a legitimate license. At the time he got his motorbike license, in the early 1930s, it was also valid to drive a motor car and he kept renewing it and was still valid in 1962. However, he had never driven a car and thus, no one to drive the car; a small oversight. But here comes cute Mother again! She remembered the husband of one of her maternal cousins, Len, who was a London bus driver! Bingo! Len agreed to teach me! He lived in Hanley Road, off Hornsey Road, opposite Marlborough Road, which led on to Holloway Road; all in London N19. Going the other way (east), Hanley Road led on to Stroud Green Road, the area in which Bob Hoskins grew up, apparently having been out with my first girlfriend, Gina Dalmasio; so the story goes. Another irony, I subsequently bumped into Gina (metaphorically, of course) whilst driving this said same car in October 1963, which developed into 'steamy' (windows) activities inside. She was now 18 and I was 19. Unbelievable really!

I will never forget the exact spot where I first caused a motor car to move, without stalling. It was on a road which was in fact a flat bridge over a railway line. The very same railway line that passed at the back of the first house, in Fairbridge Road, where I had lived until the age fourteen, also in London N19. The house where I had overcome my fear of the dark — with the obsession to buy records! As I sat in the car there was the famous Britain's factory where lead soldiers were manufactured, behind me. I had many and varied lead soldiers from the factory, acquired over a period of time by the mother of my best friend at primary school, David Saunders; she worked there. I spent many happy hours playing with my coveted lead soldiers. I think the road was called Spears Road. Then if you were to turn right at Hornsey Road, drive on a few hundred yards, you would soon come to a wide road open up on the left-hand side called Sunnyside Road. On the corner of that road is a public house by the name of the Favourite Pub; that's where Matt Monroe was 'discovered', as a singing bus conductor of the number 14 bus route from Hornsey Rise to Pimlico.

Len had planned a square route to drive around consisting of four roads of short distance. I don't think I got out of second gear. But after one hour, I knew I could do it; I could more than do it! Len was patient and firm, I liked that because I knew what was expected of me. Once I had mastered the clutch, the rest was second nature. Soon Len and I were driving all over the place. Up to Potters Bar, Barnet, Cockfosters, all posh areas in 1962. We booked my driving test for November at the Finchley Test Centre. I was confident — over confident, so I failed! Pluck it! And I knew why. Not far from the test centre in Finchley there are many small crossroads. At that time in 1962, even BEFORE yellow lines, whether they be single, double, triple or quadruple, small crossroads never had road markings with Slow or Stop. It was an unwritten law that one simply slowed down to 'take a gander'. I still remember and can take you to the exact crossroads, around the back streets of Finchley, where I failed my first test! Not only didn't I slow down, I didn't even change down from the top gear, third, to second gear. OMG! I can recall suddenly seeing, from my peripheral vision, the face of the examiner staring at me. Ouch!

Len was disappointed; he had done a good job. He said that I was good enough to drive on my own, albeit with the bright red 'L' plate still displayed but with Dad at my side, with the legit license. Due to the infamous winter of 1962-63 in the UK, my next test would not be until April '63 but after my birthday on the 5th, which meant I would be nineteen; pluck it! I wanted to pass it when I was eighteen! That was too old anyway!

I think I eventually took the test on the 19th April and passed with flying colours, which meant no adverse comments of significance. I bought Len a Ronson's lighter because he was a big, 'roll your own' man/fan, for his tuition. He gave me the true rudimentary basics for my driving expertise and future careers.

Now, I was on my own! I could do what the pluck I wanted; go where I wanted and as fast as I wanted. The road was my freedom, my mentor, my addiction, my friend and my lover! I could NOT keep off the road. I studied the road; the surface, the texture, the curvature, the camber, the sound of the tyres and drove accordingly. Speed, gear change, braking, cornering was all activated, dependent on the road surface. I could go as fast as I wanted, especially when cornering, if and only if, I could feel the road in the seat of my pants! I taught myself the value of precise gear changing to slow down and to quickly get me out of trouble and through corners faster, with more control! I loved the scream of the engine from third to second, only three gears remember; and first gear needed to be 'double de-clutched!' I read about it somewhere. I could feel and judge the rev count before I even knew about revs, or had a rev counter / meter. I think I used to come in from third to second at about 4,000 revs, enough for that model of car.

Memories of My Way!
August 1962

So here I was, a car driver/owner, loving my work and loving my football, with the '62/'63 season one week away. Life was great — and with a new girlfriend! But Mum knew me better than I knew myself. She innately knew that I was bordering on something OTT — <u>O</u>ver <u>T</u>he <u>T</u>op. Maybe it was my swagger/gait of an enlarged confidence level due to my new lifestyle; she 'smelt' something bad over the horizon. Vic Corby our old Old Boy football manager, financier and benefactor had come up with the idea of having a 'young' Old Boys reserve football team comprising of boys who had recently left school and started work. I happened to tell Fred about it and he asked if I would speak for Alan (albeit as a ringer), his eldest son, my cousin, now 1seventeenyears of age. To the age of nine, in 1953, we had all lived together in the same four-storey Victorian house at 132, Fairbridge Road, Upper Holloway, London N19. The house from which we ran for the bomb shelters and Underground Stations when the doodlebugs (V-2 rockets) were dropping on London in 1944.

'We' meant, Mrs Carnt (and she never did — she was a spinster), at the top of the house; only a gaslight and a water tap on the landing below. My mother, father and I in the middle and unbelievably, my maternal grandmother, grandfather, maternal Uncle Fred, Aunt Lil plus Alan and Philip, my cousins, all on the ground floor. Too many people and not enough space which inevitably, led to constant rowing, shouting and sometimes fighting between the adults, and us kids. I was raised in an ambience of hostility, adversity and tense atmospheres. Us three kids were taught to look after ourselves. Alan's favourite defence was to scratch my face but I always got the better of him and his brother, leading on to getting the better of other kids in the street and beyond.

Anyway, all that had been forgotten by the summer of '62 when Alan got a trial for the younger football team. Corby had organized a friendly match with the eldest Acland Burleigh School Boys Team, captained by Gil Jones, of Welsh origin, who at seventeen, was a refined and powerful left half-back. I don't know how it happened, but I got to captain the young Old Boys team. The match was played at Parliament Hill Fields, adjacent to the changing rooms. It was a bright and sunny Saturday morning; Fred and Alan had picked me up in the minivan from 42, Calverley Grove, Hornsey Rise, London N19, where we had moved to in 1958 when I was fourteen. I was feeling decidedly OTT. I was bursting with energy, enterprise and showmanship. As soon as we kicked off, I was all over the pitch, spraying passes in all directions. Over the previous ten years of playing competitive football I had played at right back, inside left, centre forward and right half-back. But today, I was my own man, placing myself in a similar role that Bobby Charlton would play, as a deep-lying centre forward — and I was loving it. At half time we were 2–0 up and I decided that I wanted to be on the score sheet and so played further up field in a more orthodox centre forward position. I remember a high ball coming over from the left wing. I burst forward from an onside position; it was just the goalie and me. My acute 'time and distance' instinct instantaneously informed me that the goalie should catch the ball just before my head would connect.

But here I am oozing with adrenalin, desperate to score and impress those watching the match. At that time, in 1962, it was still allowed to barge the goalkeeper. So, with maximum pace and momentum, I hurled myself through the air in the direction of the ball and goalie. I was nineteen, stocky, strong and all muscle. The goalie was tall, slim and a sixteen/seventeen-year-old schoolboy. I couldn't do it! As I flew through the air, I changed my body plane from horizontal to vertical to avoid colliding with the goalie. What I had forgotten, however, was the consequence of changing my mind and shape when I hit the ground. As I landed, my right shoulder took the full impact of the velocity of my body weight and momentum. The muscles cushioned some impact but the momentum travelled along my right collar bone and snapped it! I couldn't move! I was in excruciating pain, to the point of almost passing out. Even to breathe was agonizing. Suddenly, my new found lifestyle stopped — right there!

Mum intuitively knew I was in line for some kind of a 'knock-back'. That's why she didn't want me to have a scooter!

Memories of My Way
1962

At long last, after six weeks, I was back at work! The fellas were genuinely pleased to see me back and had previously, while I was off work, organized a whip round for me whereby I received the princely sum of GBP 5.00d. It's the thought that counts; but that was in 1962. Attitudes 50 plus years later had changed, completely.

Yes, I was back at work but somehow it was never the same. I think my uncle sensed something and put me with a new 'subby' team of 3+1; three brickies + one labourer. Derek, a 5'4" Welshman, was the 'lead trowel', followed by Keith and Bob, both English and then, the incomparable, Peter — an Irish 'work machine!' My God, could this man work? He was labouring to three fast trowels plus me, for what that was worth, at the age of eighteen! Derek was a ball of energy! He had vision, could organize and layout the brick/block work, led by example, would encourage and cajole and had indefatigable determination! I admired him and endeavoured to emulate him.

Bob and Keith were like university drop-outs, especially Keith who possessed the posh Surrey accent. Peter possessed manic power, strength and severe pride! For one labourer to service three (usually two) brickies was already hard to do but bricklayers of the aforementioned calibre, unbelievable; now there was little me! No probs for Peter. I recall Derek pushing me to do more and more — and more! He was a slave driver but I liked him. We worked together and we formed a bond! He even got me a pay rise, from my <u>own uncle</u>!

As we approached the winter of '62–'63 the weather became colder and colder, enough to freeze the balls off a brass monkey. The River Thames became frozen along the Sunbury area; it was quite narrow there. It became too cold to lay bricks and so there was a lot of hammer and chisel work called 'cutting away', invariably alterations made by the stroke of a pencil, from the architect. Many men were laid off in the building trade, throughout the whole country, including Dad. I managed to hang in, maybe due to my privileged position of nephew, to the contract's manager.

I used to go to work by bus and still arrive at 8.00 am, from Hornsey Rise to Sunbury-on-Thames; I forget what happened to Fred during that period. I 'worked' for two hours on site, waiting to see if the temperature would rise; if not, then I was back home, on a full day's pay!

Eventually Christmas came and went — and so did the New Year!

Little did I know that 1963 would be a life-changing year for me.

The snow and cold weather continued, men got restless, including me! Derek went off to do his own thing; Keith, Bob and Peter found another site. I remember shedding a tear as I watched them leave our site!

I think it was about mid-February '63, when temperatures began to rise. By March/April most of the bulk of brick/block work had been completed. I was doing more and more 'making good' inside; patching up holes, fixing wash hand basins, pipes and the like. Other trades were now on the site; plasterers, electricians, heating and ventilation plumbers. Unfortunately, there was one particular plumber from London that I took a distinct dislike to. He was in his early twenties, big, fat and mouthy. He was always mouthing off, taking the piss and lauding it about, by chance never to me personally. However, one day I decided that I was going to give him a taste of his own medicine both verbally and physically. He was about 6' tall and probably weighed about fifteen stone. I was never attracted to fights with men of my own size; rightly or wrongly, I always felt superior and knew I was going to win. I have never liked losing at anything and will continue until I drop. I hoarded memories of vanquished foes embedded in my sub-conscious mind and detested the look in their eyes when beaten.

I had been well trained as a kid by my father, a fighter, and paternal grandfather, amateur boxer, to look after myself! For the first nine years of my life I had always been fighting with my two cousins, until they finally left the four-storey house in which we were living at Fairbridge Road, London, N19. I had an innate sense of weight distribution, leverage, time and distance, and, I could take pain. Furthermore, I was exceptionally strong!

Memories of My Way
1962

One bright, sunny crisp morning I decided that I had had enough of Fatso by shouting out, "Hey Fatso, you fat freak. Shout your fucking mouth!" To which he turned and came for me 'f'ing and 'blindin'. We were on the ground floor of the police cadet college in an area which was to be a gymnasium; it felt right, it felt good — I felt good! I backed up against a wall, standing on the bare concrete floor in my Dr. Martens white boots, dressed in tough jeans, a warm shirt and woollen top. I was ready — I wanted it! He was big enough for me not to worry about hurting him; he was mine and he was going to get the full monty! No holds barred! I shouted further abuse at him. I wanted him mad. I wanted him as mad as bull. I wanted him 'at me, up close'. I wanted him to throw the first punch; I wanted him to punch the wall. And he did — throw a punch but he was faster than I thought because as I ducked under his outstretched arm, his fist curled down and fortunately hit fresh air. As I had quickly side-stepped to my left, I planted a 'haymaker' in his 'bread-basket'; a short half uppercut bang into his solar plexus using the power of my immensely strong stomach muscles and using the balls of my feet as a fulcrum and extra leverage to dig deep. To accelerate his fall, with the outside blade of my right foot, I slammed it against the back of his knee. He went down like a sack of the proverbial! As he rolled on the concrete floor, I dive bombed him right in the middle of his gut. I heard air hissing out of his mouth, just like a steam engine. I quickly levered myself over his large torso and thrust the outside blade of my forearm under his blubberous chin, hard against his throat, with all my might! His tongue and eyes popped. He was struggling with arms flaying all over the place but with no power. I was up in his face and tempted to head butt it, but the angle and distance did not feel right. The last thing I remember was the desire to stop him moving. Then, suddenly, I was landing on the hard concrete a few feet away. I had been grabbed, picked up and thrown across the floor by a number of workmen who had been watching. I later learned that I was actually trying to finish Fatso off!

The site came to a temporary standstill with Fatso being taken off to, I don't know where; I never saw him again. I think my uncle banned him from the site. But he also gave me a rollicking, which upset me; I felt that I had let him down. Within two weeks, I was also off the site.

Memories of My Way
Spring/Summer 1963

During the long hours working on the Ronson site at Leatherhead, Surrey, I had slipped into a similar mindset as that when I was working at Ernest F. Moy, Camden Town, three years earlier — I got to thinking and dreaming. With the life-changing capability and thrill of driving a car on my own, new thoughts were altering my outlook on life. I had been gearing myself up to make the building trade my life, albeit as a contracts' manager, director of a construction company, maybe a brickwork subcontractor; establishing my own construction company and travelling around the world laying bricks and chicks! "Have Trowel — Will Travel." I had been extremely focused and determined causing my learning curve to go exponential. But now, with the limitless freedom which the automobile offered, my dreams rose far beyond the horizon. Gifted (and burdened) with boundless energy, the automobile awakened the restless giant, within me.

In July/August 1963 Corby had organized for the original old Boys Football team to play in Tarragona Spain; at least I had that to look forward to. But before that and quite out of the blue, I had an inspiration — "Let's drive to Cornwall" for a holiday and challenge (or was it the other way around?). Whilst attending the infants' at Duncombe Road School, London N19, circa 1949/51, Mum had befriended the mother of one of the other boys, Brian, same age as me and also living in Fairbridge Rd. N19, virtually opposite Ashbrook Road, the posher end, closer to Holloway Road. Actually, opposite the large corner house where the 'Bachelors', three singing Irish brothers who had hits in the 60s, lived. During 1950, Elsie, Brian and Bob, his father, had decided to move to Cornwall, to St. Austell to be exact. They had a plan to buy up old caravans, renovate them and then let them out to holidaymakers in the summer. Bob went first and got a job as a milkman, then Brian and Elsie, his mother, followed. Ten years later they had accumulated enough money to buy a run-down pseudo mansion house in several acres of countryside land, overlooking Pentewan Sands between St. Austell and Mevagissey for just a few thousand pounds. They converted the flat land at the front into a caravan park plus facilities, amenities and recreations. They named it — Sun Valley Caravan Park.

"Let's ring Elsie, Brian and Bob and stay at their caravan park for a week," says I.

Mum and Dad were taken aback but I got it all agreed and organized. Alan, my cousin, was to join us. Dad wrote to the A.A. (Automobile Association) for an itinerary all the way to St. Austell, which was brilliant. I was the driver and Dad, the navigator. We fixed a roof-rack to the roof of the Ford Escort for additional luggage and covered it with canvass tarpaulin; we then strapped it down with rope and elasticised hooks. Imagine, an 1100 cc engine pulling four adults plus luggage at the back and on the roof, two hundred and fifty miles; I think it took us ten hours plus. Later, in 1967, I drove my black MG Midget, also 1100cc, Bermuda hard-top from Hornsey Rise to Newquay, North Devon in four and three-quarter hours, 288 minutes, stopping only once to refuel. No motorways in that direction then. When I arrived in Newquay, my whole body was shaking with excessive adrenalin.

Back to '63. I don't remember much of the holiday in terms of where we went (apart from Porlock Hill), but what I do remember was Brian and his two-litre Triumph Vitesse V6 and his immaculate driving skills. As he entered corners his brake lights did not come on. He drove through the corners like a Scalextric toy car; smooth and fast. Eventually I figured out what he was doing — using gears to slow him down, affording him more control when manoeuvring corners. This one observation improved my driving skills immeasurably! I later spoke to Brian and he revealed that he had been rally-driving around the lanes and countryside of Cornwall since he was sixteen.

After a week we were all safely back in London without any adverse motoring incidents. However, about two weeks later, I did experience my first (one of many) motoring incidents. An incident of adversity, which would turn into a seed of opportunity and change my life!

Memories of My Way!
Summer of '63

The summer of '63 saw us Old Boys playing football in Tarragona, Spain, South of Barcelona. Corby, our benevolent, old, Old Boy manager had arranged for us to play the Tarragona 'A' Team plus another game somewhere near Barcelona. We summarily lost both matches. We had travelled by ship, from England to France, then by train, across France to the border with Spain. Then, on and on, diagonally across Spain to Terragona, on the mid-east coast — standing — all the way!

    I loved the excitement and sensation of playing on a full-size football pitch plus a crowd of spectators, albeit small, with floodlights an' all. This ambiance caused me to rise above the occasion. I knew I was going to play out of my skin and EVERYONE was going to remember ME! I commenced to visualize my Dave McKay mind-set but harder. I was feeling <u>so</u> strong, tough, indestructible and uncompromising! 1963 was before yellow / red cards; football was still a contact sport for men, so I could legitimately, do what I loved- crunching tackles. I had perfected sliding tackles, ball first, then the player, up in the air. I had/have a low centre of gravity and have always been muscular and heavy at 5'7"; difficult to knock over. The larger opponents were the ones that went, 'up and over', the best!

The outcome of my going to Spain just intensified my restless nature. I came to realise that there was another world beyond the shores of England. Beyond the shores of good ol' Blighty. There were people with different values, attitudes, work ethics, food, drink, who enjoyed life in a different and happier way; in a less reserved and stressful way. In a way whereby they had more time for each other. And that was in 1963! What's it like now? I did not want to go back home but how to stay by?

In retrospect it would have been easy for me to stay in Spain. Tarragona F.C. had made overtures to me about my 'no-nonsense' style of play but I was naïve and ignorant of such matters and so bowed to the flock syndrome and dutifully returned to ol' Blighty.

Memories of My Way!
August 1963

So, when I got back home, the inevitable happened — that's right — I was bored out of my brains! Within two weeks of returning to Ronson's site, I quit! The site was not ready for brickies but my Uncle Fred wanted me off the Sunbury site due the incident with the big fat arsehole plumber from London. So, I was killing time, something that I am not very good at doing, waiting for the foundations to be dug out for the new building. A part of the existing structure was to remain to be refurbished, so I was 'making good' here and 'cutting away' there; doing a bit of brickwork here, building a pier or two there. One day, I was given the task of cutting away excess concrete off a pile emerging from below ground level. I was down in a large hole (never been attracted to large holes ever since), cutting away concrete with a 5lb club hammer and cold steel chisel. Suddenly I was overcome by a feeling of acute psychological claustrophobia; a similar feeling as I experienced whilst working at Ernest F. Moy's factory in Camden Town. "What am I doing here? In a hole cutting away concrete; you must be mad!" I cast my mind back to my days at my beloved school, Acland Central Boy's School, London NW5 and the great education I had received. But moreover, nagging at me from the back of my mind, was the Escort, sitting on the road, outside the site — doing — nothing! I had taken to driving the pale blue Escort to Leatherhead, Surrey from Hornsey Rise, every day. I wanted to be like Michael, my second cousin. I wanted to be an insurance agent! (As a point of interest, another second cousin of mine, the son of Lilian, Maude's sister is/was, Anthony Newlands, a British actor on TV; he had a regular series, acting as a judge.

Meanwhile, back in the hole, I was imagining driving around the streets of North and North West London, calling on customers to collect premiums, do business to be free and independent. Suddenly, I was out of the hole and in front of the site agent telling him to, "Lick 'em and stick 'em!" A building trade euphemism which eased the (possible) unpleasant decision of leaving — 'jacking up!'

Leaving at the end of the week or, there and then (as I did). The licking and the sticking was the act of bringing one's National Insurance Stamps up to date, by the employer, in one's National Insurance stamp book. My decision to 'jack up' took everyone by surprise, especially Fred!

I was to become an insurance agent — I had created the desire — now, I will make it come true. I had decided! In August 1963, I was approaching nineteen and a half years of age. How could I do that? How DID I do that? I was, even then, subconsciously using, the power of visualisation!

"Whatever the mind can conceive and believe — it can

achieve!"

Michael had already spoken to Mr Martin, the 'B' divisional manager of the London and Manchester Assurance Company Ltd. at the regional offices in Seven Sisters Road, N4 (opposite Finsbury Park, on the other side of the road) about the prospect of my becoming an insurance agent, even though the minimum age was twenty-one!

Mr Martin, Leslie Martin, was of the old, old school, immaculately dressed. He wore pinstripe trousers, white shirt (hard-collar), silver-grey tie, black waistcoat, light-weight, three quarter open, smock-like (similar to the length that artists traditionally wore) black top and black sparkling shoes. He spoke with a cultured English accent — almost; I detected a timbre of conscious development, and not inherent. (Perhaps, "workin' class boy dun well") I liked that. He was positive, forceful but graciously charming — obviously a great salesman. He oozed confidence, experience and determination. And — most importantly, I liked him. He was a leader by example! During the interview he would quickly switch his boundless charm into polite, direct and confrontational questions and statements. Michael had warned me that he, Mr Martin, would tease out my true character and test my resolve with a confrontational attitude. I was up for it!

"Well Mr Tetlow (I was only nineteen, and being addressed as Mr Tetlow, as in, "With respect Sir!" — then a barrage of confrontational innuendos shooting out of his mouth, straight into my face), the conclusion I have come to is that you, Mr Tetlow are lazy! The building trade has become too hard for you and you now see yourself as an insurance agent, driving around in your car, not doing much!"

Michael appears in my mind's eye. "Calm down, Bernard!"

"No Mr Martin, I am not lazy! I see Mr Redman (Michael) doing well as an insurance agent and improving himself after leaving the building trade and I want to do the same."

Not bad for a nineteen-year-old, eh? Especially in 1963!

"Well, as you have shown a keen interest and enthusiasm to become an insurance agent with the London and Manchester, I will put your application forward to the directors at head office in Finsbury Square." (City of London) Mr Martin must have liked me as well because a week later I was summoned back to the divisional office for a second interview. Mr Martin informed me that I had been accepted by the directors (humbug — it was him) for a six-month probationary period as an insurance agent on the B.16.2. debit. This was now September 1963; seven months later on my twentieth birthday, 5th April 1964, I bought a brand new 850cc white Mini super-de-luxe car! ALU 26B.

(Super-de-luxe meant I got a heater, a water gauge, an oil gauge and superior upholstery. It cost me GBP 493.00p!

Memories of MY WAY! September/ October 1963

So here I was, a nineteen and a half-year-old insurance agent. Mum said that I would need to make myself look older. So Mum, Dad and I went down to Petticoat Lane market to buy some clothes. We got off the bus at Finsbury Square, ironically passing the London and Manchester head office, to cut through to Petticoat Lane. Dad knew the streets of London like the back of his hand; 'traipsing around in the 20s, 30s, 40s and beyond looking for work. Knocking on yet another building site door, approaching a bricklayer foreman, "How yer fixed for brickies?" My dad had to find his own work; maybe that's why I have never been scared to, knock on doors!

Petticoat Lane market, in East London was renowned for the place where you could buy anything, even a monkey, if you were so inclined. The fellas selling out of the backs of lorries were a sight to be seen and heard — amazing salesmen. But I was here to buy a Trilby hat and an overcoat and I wanted dark blue! I had already bought a new three-piece suit from Burton's at the Archway, N19, even before the one-way system was instituted.

The suit was also dark blue with faint silvery stripes; three-piece meaning, inclusive of waistcoat. Was I 'Jack the Lad'! or was I 'Jack the Lad'? I WAS Jack the Lad.

My training with L&M lasted one week, out on the debit with my manager, Ernie Boudier, an ex-milkman, full of cheek and personality — old style.

He was the manager of Highgate District 16; Mr Martin was the 'B' divisional manager of the country; I was given the number 2 area of the Highgate District. So, my agency number was B.16.2. — never forget it. My debit/agency area covered parts of London N7, N19 and NW5.

The first thing I did was to buy an A-Z street map of London to enable me to outline the boundaries of my debit. When I had finished, I gazed down and as my eyes followed the boundary and I recognized virtually all the roads, I was filled with excitement and responsibility. This was MY area; MY

Debit; MY Business; MY Field! (Recommend that you watch the DVD — *The Field*, starring Richard Harris. A brilliant film about misguided arrogance and blind-faith belief.)

My responsibilities as B.16.2 were to collect cash premiums for life assurance/insurance plus car insurance, travel insurance, home contents, building insurance, ire insurance, in fact, whatever insurance had been and could be sold. London and Manchester covered them all. As a point of interest, life assurance is paid out on death, over an open-ended period of time. Life insurance is paid out within a specified term of years.

Every week I had to account, to the last ha' penny, for all my collections — before I got paid! And — no calculators then! Other responsibilities were to pay out death claims and the maturity of savings plans. Also, complete the fire and general claims and make recommendations as to the credibility of any said claims and amount to be paid out. I remember very early on, still in '63, one of the clients of L&M had returned from their holidays to find that their flat had been burgled; they were on to me about a claim. I told Mr Boudier, my manager, who gave me a form for completion. In retrospect it must have been quite comical, a youth of nineteen plus asking the family, "What happened?" "What's missing?" "Where have you been?"

Memories of My Way!
September/ October 1963

Eventually an offer came down from the head office less than the claim. So, the family are unto me, again. Back to Mr Boudier at the office, who gives me a more complex form to complete. This time I have to give a sworn affidavit that I believe the story to be true; which I did. The family got the full claim paid out! Guess what, after the pay-out I did a lot of business with various members of the family. That's when I first learned about service, "Give, before you take!" So, from then on, I looked for opportunities where I could be of help and service; the new business just followed on. I can still remember my first pension sale; it was to a man in his late thirties and I was still nineteen! He said, "I want to save some money for when I retire. You're a bright young man, what do you suggest? (Bright young man?)" I had heard Mr Martin going on about pension plans but I didn't really know what he was talking about. However, I could give the answer to expected returns on premiums paid over given terms of years, there and then — without a computer or calculator! Why!

Because I had a black leather-bound rate book (given to all agents), inside of which was relevant information regarding all the insurances which L&M transacted, inclusive of fire and general.

"How much a week can you put aside?" asks I. Then I would flick through and select the correct page, run along the charts/lines of premiums invested against term of years and, 'Hey Presto!' there was the answer. No concern about, 'Poor signal!' 'Computer is down! Closed! At the point of desire! (Oh! Sorry darling, "My Computer is going down, can you wait a few minutes, until it's up again?") This was even before, wait for it… calculators! The era to which I am referring is when people knew how to USE the greatest computer EVER created — or will be created! My calculations of premiums collected for the week. albeit collecting every denomination of the English currency, at that time, were done in MY BRAIN!

I couldn't believe that I had sold a pension plan to a man twenty years older than me. My confidence level went into orbit!

Being a nineteen to twenty-year-old insurance agent exposed me to many temptations, especially in the direction of lonely and bored housewives, many still in their twenties. I was forever being invited in for cups of tea and crumpet.

I was apprehensive at first but I knew Michael was having a lot of fun with various housewives and cajoled me to do the same. He was already married with far more experience than me and so therefore he could handle married women but not me, at this stage. However, around October '63, I decided to take on a sixteen-year-old schoolgirl who had been introduced to me. I used to pick her up from her school in my car, before my Monday evening collections. She was petite, blond hair, beautiful blue eyes, rosy cheeks and ample body — great butt!

We used to drive off somewhere secluded, still in her school uniform and use the time saved from her usual mode of transport, to play. She was cute, sexy and naughty. Although only sixteen she was sexually liberated, agreeable and receptive; especially receptive. I became well-versed in the art of cunnilingus, that well-known Irish Airline. Sometimes we would get back to her house early, straight from school and sit on the sofa. It was quite arousing having a schoolgirl, still in her uniform, panties on the floor, with her naked butt perched on the edge of the sofa and her legs on my shoulders, munching at her young femininity. Is that what is called — succumbing?

My first married lover was just around the corner — literally! Guess who?

Memories of My Way!
Autumn 1963

Ironically, at that time of 'playing' with the sixteen-year-old schoolgirl, I bumped into Gina! Yes! Gina Dalmasio. I hadn't seen her for three years (she was 18 now) but had heard that she had been making lots of friends, including Bob Hoskins of *'Long Good Friday'* fame. He originated from Stroud Green, between Hornsey Rise and Finsbury Park. But now, she (Gina) was married to a previous primary school friend, Vicky Long, who was a bit of a bully at school but a great, natural swimmer. It was Vic Long who precipitated my short-lived reign as somewhat of a school hero in 1955. What led to this, legend in my own school (tea) break fame, was a scuffle with the classroom prefect, David Portch, who, unbelievably, would subsequently court Gina when we were at the Acland Burghley and, believe it or not, she would marry (after Vic), Harry Mead, who sat at the back desk in the same row as me in the primary school. Harry's sister, Mary, was the best friend of Janet, the sister of Michael Redman. Portch was the favourite of Mr Stanley, our class master. Stanley caught Portch and me rolling around the corridor floor, fighting, as the class queued to go into the classroom. Stanley pulled me off Portch and marched me to my desk. There was deathly silence as Stanley spoke out and said something along the lines that due to my misbehaviour, he would make sure that I would not play football for the school team that afternoon. I burst into tears! Then, I heard a whisper from behind me. It was Longy: "If you can't play football, then Portch should have his prefect's badge taken away!" The next thing I knew, I was on my feet screaming the very same words, verbatim at Stanley. This behaviour was unheard of in 1955, just ten years after the end of WWII, especially from an eleven-year-old! Stanley, who had a stiff leg and supporting stick, came hopping across the classroom towards me. I stood there and just looked at him; he gave me an almighty smack across the face then grabbed me and marched me off to the headmaster's office. What would become of me? Mr Taylor, the headmaster, was a quiet, genteel man who prompted me to reveal the problem. When I put my case forward between sobs of mixed emotions, he said, "Don't worry Tetlow, you can still play football for the school this afternoon." Immediately, I was released from my disappointment, worry and anxiety.

By now it was playtime and as I walked out of the school building and onto the landing and steps leading down to the playground, I saw a sea of faces looking up to me, with expressions of admiration, shouting, "'He's got STUG! He's got STUG! He's got STUG!" Stug being the word contrived by our music teacher, Mr Rodney for those boys who had the GUTS (STUG) to get up and sing! I was a hero! I'd had the audacity to stand up to a formidable teacher at the tender age of ten or eleven years of age. As I walked down the stone steps, some boys grabbed me and put me on their shoulders and paraded me around the playground like a victorious general returning home from battle. I enjoyed the adulation but it did not impact on me long term, but in retrospect, I would have liked it to have done. That afternoon, the school football team went on to win the match 3-2, with yours truly scoring two goals!

So, Vicky Long had already influenced my life and now he was married to my first dated girlfriend. And so, here we are in November 1963, four years to the day, almost, from my first date with Gina! 11th November 1959.

So, here I am driving along Harberton Road, N19; the road in which Gina lives in the corner house with Cressida Road, which leads up to Hornsey Lane; number 109, to be exact! Suddenly I see her pushing a pram along the pavement. As I see her, she sees me — and bingo! Right there, at that split second, as our eyes meet, the attraction is reborn — instantaneously! It was a little awkward because we were both feeling the same feelings but trying to hide them. She told me what I had previously heard on the grapevine that she was now married to Vicky Long — I took this as a 'back-off' sign — but it was to be subsequently proven not to be so. We exchanged further pleasantries but no plans were made to meet up again. When I got home later in the day, Mum said, "You're never going to guess who came here this afternoon — Gina!"

Memories of My Way!

The last event I recall of 1963 is one of a comedy of contradictions, the outcome of which was that I earned in excess of GBP 30.00 — in one week! And that was the last week before Christmas! This sum was twice the amount Dad was earning, still working on the sites, at age fifty. Probably more than Uncle Fred, albeit still contracts manager for Gazes on the Ronson's site, at Leatherhead, Surrey.

It was unheard of in 1963, especially for a nineteen-year-old!

It would only have been GBP 20.00, if not for Corby; Mr Corby, Mr Vic Corby, our football mentor, organiser, manager, who did some insurance business with me in December, which earned me GBP10.00! He had known me as a bricklayer and a loyal team member of the original Old Boy's football team, having broken my collar bone whilst showing off to Fred and Alan, who were playing for the YOBs (Young Old Boys' team); having only, four months earlier, returned from playing football in Spain, for the Old Boys. Now, here he (Corby) was writing out a cheque in the sum of GBP 100.00

to London & Manchester Ass. Co. Ltd. as the first annual premium of a ten-year pension plan. I was excited! I was proud! I was nineteen!

Many years later I recalled that nostalgic moment and came to the conclusion that Vic Corby admired me for what I was doing. I had been working in the building trade, but got out! Corby was still working in the building trade, albeit as a director of his own heating and ventilating company in Farringdon Street, London, EC1. So here comes this nineteen and a half-year-old whipper snapper, who is not only out of the building trade but now growing a successful insurance business AND earning more money! Corby knew that, and as a seasoned businessman himself, admired what I had done, and was now doing. Ironically, Reggie Bacchus was working for Corby and it was Reggie's sister, Marion, to whom I was 'succumbing!' Funny ol' world!

Memories of My Way!
1964

As always, Christmas and the New Year came and went, as they always do. In early '64, I succumbed no more. Well, not with Marion, anyway. Gina had been simmering on the back burner for quite a while, to the point of, 'boiling over!' I didn't want her over-boiled and dried up, so I decided it was time to eat — her! Ever since that first encounter, a few weeks earlier of bumping into her along Harberton Road, London, N19, she had taken it upon herself to frequent 42, Calverley Grove, N19 with her baby daughter, on the pretence of seeing Mum, but ostensibly, to see me. We became tactile in a playful, teasing mode but no intimacy or even kissing; Mum was always there. So I decided to pop the question about having a clandestine friendship, inclusive of sexual relations — she agreed! Another irony was that we arranged to meet the next Wednesday evening, which was the same day of our first date, on 11th November 1959, fifty months earlier. She was now married to Vicky Long, the boy in the same class as I, at Duncombe Road School, N19, in 1955. I was consumed with the UNKNOWN! An insatiable curiosity. An unbelievable mixture of varying feelings. Overall, I felt compelled to overcome and taste fear, desire, excitement and Gina's 'charms!'

We arranged to meet at the top of Cressida Road, N19, which actually is a steep, hilly road, leading to Hornsey Lane. And, unbelievably, the same road where we had arranged to meet on our very first date on 11th November 1959 but that time, at the bottom of Cressida Road. Hornsey Lane being the northern boundary between the Borough of Islington and Hornsey. We then drove off to Epping Forest. I still had the Ford Escort at that time and although not ideal, "Where there's a will, there's a way!" Well I certainly had the will (throbbing!) and Gina certainly had THE way (in)! She always was a hot young girl, even at fourteen but now, now, at age 18, she was a scorching young woman; far more experienced than me but I wasn't complaining. She took over and did whatever came into her fertile imagination to do. As the spring and summer drew near, we would drive out to St. Albans on a Thursday and find a quiet, shady nook to relax and play; it was nice and civilized. We had fun together; the problem was, we genuinely liked each other too much. We HAD to be careful and thank God, we were.

A few years later I heard that Gina and Vic had divorced and that Gina had married Harry Mead. Harry being another member of the 'Class of 4', in 1955. The four being Dave Portch, the first to court Gina in October 1959 when Acland Central Boy's School, NW5, merged with Burghley School, NW5, which was mixed, boys and girls. Then second, me, in

November 1959; third, Vicky Long, married; fourth Harry Mead, married. Ironic — right? Yet another irony. Harry Mead was the boy who, in February 1957, passed over his paper round to me at the age of twelve! And it was the money I earned from that paper round, which gave me the opportunity to take Gina to the Astoria Picture Palace, Finsbury Park, N4, on 11th November 1959, when this book first commenced! How amazing is that? And Mary, Harry's elder sister, was friends with Janet, the younger sister of Michael, who had introduced me to L&M!

Memories of My Way
Summer/Autumn 1964

Life was great! Life was fun! I was earning far more money than I needed. I had a new car, new clothes, a regular sex-gig; my social skills and confidence levels were soaring sky high and I was still only twenty years of age!

"Door knocking" was paying off!

In retrospect, I should have bought a house with my parents; I could afford it, plus London and Manchester had a great concession on interest rates for employees. But in 1964 houses were owned by a different, socio-economic strata, to that of which my family belonged that would be going too far Bernard, or so I thought.

However, as the year passed by, a large negative cloud loomed above us. Mum tells me I will soon have a baby brother or sister! What? Mum was born in 1916 and although extremely gregarious, perceptive and philosophical, she was somewhat naïve about taboo subjects such as the workings of the human body. In the summer of '64 Mum was forty-seven and a half years of age and close to her menopause. When, in fact, her menstrual cycle came to an end, in her naïve thinking — she was pregnant! However, even on the realization that she was not pregnant and therefore relieved, Mum was never the same again. Her whole demeanour changed. She suddenly had numerous outbursts of crying fits. She became depressed and began to despise her surroundings and wanted out — out of 42, Calverly Grove, out of the area; out of London!

She concluded that council accommodation was the answer and so we marched off to the nearest and most appropriate Council Offices. When the council employees tried to 'fob her off' they were suddenly on the end of a verbal whipping! Mum cited many examples of others who were living in council property, who, in her mind, were not deserving; none less than those from other countries. Her perception, verbal skill and ability to counter ANYTHING the council people said with machine-gun rapidity, was causing the council representatives to recoil in shock and embarrassment. She made them find a way and was subsequently given three council house locations from which to choose. One was in London. "No!" Sudbury? "No!" Aylesbury, Bucks? "Yes!"

The deal was that Dad, at age fifty-one, would travel to and from London to Aylesbury every day to work on a new site from 8:00 am to 5:00 pm, then back to Hornsey Rise. A daunting chore for anyone!

Mum was the mouth — Dad was the muscle.

We eventually moved to Aylesbury on 5th January 1965.

Memories of My Way!
1965

Aylesbury, Buckinghamshire in 1965 was still quaint and rural. London and Manchester had offered me a debit area out of the Luton, Beds, office which covered Dunstable, Leighton Buzzard, including Linslade, the town where the Great Train Robbery had taken place two years earlier, plus the surrounding villages. I liked my new post from a driving point of view, due to the rural road challenges of differing terrain, road surfaces and tight corners; but for writing new business, I was going down the tubes, big time!

The villagers were fascinated by my London dress, attitude and accent, especially the females, some of whom were coming on to me but I did not respond. Females and sex still represented danger to me at that time. Some of the villagers were quite quaint with broad country accents, simple and naïve in many aspects. I detected an element of inter-breeding which produced a number of simpletons in various families. My new lifestyle was interesting, informative and entertaining at times but overall, I was losing my enthusiasm for my work.

Furthermore, there was apprehension of doing business with a "City Slicker!"

By March I was down but not out! Mr Martin the 'B' Divisional Manager tried to rescue the situation by introducing me to the High Wycombe manager but to no avail; my enthusiasm had gone. New surroundings, new lifestyle and now a man at age twenty-one had caused me to become restless and distracted from my obsession of the year before — my career as an insurance agent. Suddenly the world was a much bigger place with so much to see, experience to do and learn; so much variety and curiosity.

Whilst in High Wycombe, I had noticed a branch of the British School of Motoring. My new obsession was driving motor cars — fast! Driving eventually took over my life! In the meantime, I left good old L&M and joined the United Friendly Ass. Co. Ltd. I was working out of an office in Aylesbury, so much closer to home, with a debit, predominantly at the Royal Air Force camp living quarters in Wendover Bucks. What a shower of debauched, grubby and narrow-minded people the clients were. My sales figures were virtually non-existent. I had lost the plot.

Memories of My Way!
Second Quarter 1965

My fertile brain began working overtime and it decided that I was to become a Driving Instructor for the British School of Motoring at the tender age of twenty-one! So, I drove off to High Wycombe and boldly introduced myself to the BSM manager. He subsequently took me out for a test drive around the streets of High Wycombe and approved of my driving technique, albeit, "A bit on the fast side!" He, then and there, booked me into the next session at the BSM Test Centre for Driving Instructors at Putney, South West London. And now on the BSM course, I was, by far, the youngest there. But of, course, I was one of the first to pass, first time!

And soon I was off to my chosen BSM branch at St. Albans, Herts. The idea was to commute, every day, back and forth to Aylesbury; a total of seventy miles plus, every day. Ironically, however, on my very first lesson, the tuition car got a puncture. The branch manager was not impressed and I was immediately transferred to the Golders Green branch in North West London. So, here comes the biggest irony of all. The answer to — where am I going to live?

Answer — 42 Calverley Grove and to live with my grandparents! In less than six months I had gone 360 degrees — from number 42 and then back again! On one hand it cost me a career focus but on the other, I had accelerated my maturity level and confidence via unusual circumstances and knowledge for a twenty-one-year-old, in 1965. Additional barriers were pushed further when BSM asked me to teach in Ipswich for one week, staying in creepy lodgings. Mum said, "I don't know what's gonna happen to you; you can't carry on like this!" The words were delivered in such a way that made me think that I was doing something wrong. Actually, I would have been happy being a 'floater' for BSM, floating from branch to branch, around the country; instead number 42 was seen to be the better bet, even though it was a blow to Mum. Not only was her only child not living with her for the first time in her life but I had defected to the 'other side' by going back to live at number 42. In my mind I was not doing that, I just needed to have somewhere to live, to eat and have my clothes washed. No washing machines at home in those days; well not in our family, anyway. Launderettes were few and far between and I had never even been inside one. Men didn't do that sort of thing, then. Women hand-washed at home. So, in the light of my ignorance and inability to look after myself domestically, I moved back!

Memories of My Way
September 1965

After a short while in my new position as a driving instructor for the British School of Motoring, I decided to take my Advanced Driving Test. I met the examiner at Rickmansworth train station, Herts; an ex-police driver. He directed me all around the surrounding areas; Watford, Bushey, Eastedte, Harrow, Northwood, Heathrow, it went on and on, I did not stop driving! I was asked to conduct a running commentary on what I was observing as I drove; also "What was the last sign you just passed?" Driving, in and out of varying speed limits, with little time to adjust; congested areas; high concentration of pedestrians; awkward turns, reversing around corners, uphill; three-point turn in confined space/narrow streets; driving at speed; emergency stop — you name it. I passed with flying colours! One criticism, which I cajoled out of the examiner, was that on one occasion I should have used the horn.

So here I am, a driving instructor for BSM, an Advanced Motorist and not yet twenty-one and a half years of age. Then, within two weeks of passing my Advanced Driving Test I was accused of being the culprit of a five-vehicle crash! The time was 8:00-8:15 am on a wet September morning. I was on the outside lane of slow-moving traffic, approaching the Spaniard's Inn, along Spaniard's Lane from East to West. I was preparing to turn right into Winnington Road, just up from Bishops' Avenue, 'Millionaire's Row'. The slow-moving traffic was caused by the bottleneck, in close proximity of the Spaniard's Inn building on one side of the road and a one-storey small brick-built structure on the other side. Inside that structure is where, reputedly, Dick Turpin, the famous English Highwayman, had hidden from the pursuit of the law, on his famous ride, by horse, to York. Due to its historical nostalgia, the structure has preservation orders for it not to be demolished. And because it is closely adjacent to the Spaniard's Inn Tavern, the space between is not conducive for two vehicles to pass at the same time — hence, a bottleneck.

I was now in position to turn right into Winnerton Road, Hampstead Garden Suburbs, London NW6. However, at that point the road bears sharply to the left and uphill. My Mini had a bonnet about two feet long, so therefore not an excessive protrusion.

My head was over the steering wheel, straining to see up the road, looking for cars coming the other way. As the left-hand front elevation of the Mini emerged beyond the line of traffic I suddenly saw a car, out of control, skidding past me, smashing into a Bentley emerging from Winnington Road! The impact was so great that it knocked the Bentley back into the car behind! In the next instant I was aware of another skidding car, smashing into the car in front of me. What the **** is happening? I got out of my Mini to see if anyone was injured. After a while they all picked on me as the culprit. What the **** are you talking about? My car was not touched. My take on what caused the accident.

There is always a queue of traffic, either side of that bottleneck. From east to west there is a rising incline. From west to east, there is a sloping decline. Furthermore, from west to east, there is a vicious reverse camber — and there is a signpost to that effect. September is an infamous month for accidents caused by skidding. Why? Heat from the summer sun causes small deposits of tyre rubber to adhere to the road surface. Rainfall exacerbates the slipperiness and quite often there are autumn leaves on the road surface. These three ingredients concocted a recipe for disaster, slipping and sliding on a veritable ice rink!

I believe that both drivers who lost control of their vehicles had become impatient, waiting to get through the bottleneck. When eventually through, they both put the pedal to the metal and gave no consideration to nature's challenges set before them. Then, on first sighting of the Bentley and myself, they panicked and slammed on the brakes. With the brakes locked on, they and their vehicles were out of control and both took a line of least resistance and most velocity, plus increased momentum, due to the reverse camber. Notwithstanding, I was summoned to Highgate Magistrates Court, opposite Highgate Woods, just down the road from where Rod Stewart used to live. I was represented by a retired solicitor from the Automobile Association; an elderly gentleman who advised me to plead guilty. Apparently, the person in the Bentley was the Ambassador from "Timbuktu" and had diplomatic immunity. My solicitor told me to ask for time to pay, which I did and got it. A great lesson was learned, in that respect. I got done for 'Without due Care and Attention!' HUMBUG!

Memories of My Way! Autumn 1965

I cannot remember my very first pupil at the BSM (British School of Motoring) Golders Green branch, but I do remember a few. The first I remember was a man in his mid-thirties who advised me that he previously driven but a few years ago. After the first lesson I told him he would need another six lessons to pass his test. He was amazed at the few lessons prescribed, even more amazed when he passed! Much to the chagrin of the BSM office manager. At that time, in my naivety I believed that driving schools were there to teach people to drive and make some money; not to make money in the hope that some pupils would pass their test — eventually! Another pupil was a lady around 4'11" tall. She had failed twelve driving tests! After a few minutes of driving around, I soon found out why — she had no confidence in her clutch control, especially on a hill start. So, off to Muswell Hill (London N10) we go. We drove to the back, hilly streets that fall away from Highgate Woods, down to Crouch End. There are some of the steepest hills in London. OMG! I recall the expression of fear on her face when I asked her to stop on one of the steepest!

No need to keep stalling so I advised her that I would, initially, 'feather the clutch' of the dual controls, until she got the hang of it! That she would transmute her feeling of anxiety into sensitivity; to feel and experience the subtleness of the clutch movement to remain static, on the steep incline. Clutch down, engage first gear. Set the gas! The equivalent of 1000 revs, but no rev counter. With practice the ear will identify the change of sound at the point the gears engage. When that happens, keep both feet, on the clutch and gas pedals, still! Now — release the hand break! OMG! Nerve-racking. Hold! Hold! Hold! (Mel Gibson, Braveheart) Now, slowly increase the gas and raise the clutch until the car moves, then hold both pedals, at that point.

Well, after numerous attempts/stalls over three two-hour lessons — she got it! I made her concentrate hard, but she was loving the discipline (as most females do!). A few weeks later, she went on to pass her thirteenth test.

Another pupil was a nice boy from Golders Green, always immaculately dressed, drenched in Aqua de Silva deodorant. He took longer to teach. Primarily because he was more interested in and distracted by what his style of driving looked like. Then there were two Jewish girls; one looked like Bridget Bardot, eighteen and the other, twenty-one, like Peter Sellers; in short, I lost both of 'em! I asked Bridget for a date, she told her father who complained to the management. They found her another instructor. Peter Sellers was unbelievably stupid. She was the kind of person who thought 'time and distance' was something that was taught at a university. She was the arty pseudo-intelligent kind. She held the knob of the gearstick as if she was picking up a bone china cup of tea — and when she couldn't move it, she would turn her face to me with such a look of despair. The contorted expressions on her face would cause me to laugh so much, that I was in fear of not catching my breath; a gaze of a Cheshire cat and Tommy Cooper!

We amicably agreed to part company.

Then there was a positive and attractive 40-plus-year-old Jewish business lady. She appeared more interested in me, than learning to drive; riding was more up her street! By the middle of the second lesson we were back at her house in Golders Green, drinking tea and eating cake. She knew what she wanted and it wasn't too long before she had it, in the palm of her hand. She had a nice house and appeared to live on her own. First off, I showed my apprehension with her; she was understanding, persuasive and provocative. She seduced me, and I succumbed to her charms, maturity and femininity. She was also understanding, as a young man, of my shortcomings but amazed and pleased at my prolific recovery rate.

Then there were the twins, a boy and a girl. Twins adopted by an elderly couple, out of Hampstead Garden Suburbs, one of the richest areas of London. They were both just eighteen years of age, intelligent, with a posh accent, keen and willing to learn, especially the girl. The boy was a natural driver — the girl, hesitant but safe. After a while she asked if I did lessons on a Sunday. Typically, I had not but she promised a three-hour session — what?

Most lessons were of one-hour duration with the occasional two-hour stint but NEVER three hours. Those in the office seemed to know more than me saying. "We think she likes you." She was attractive with an angelic face, round rosy cheeks, blue eyes, blond hair and plumpish, albeit young, body. Whilst I was trying to figure out how to fill a three-hour driving lesson, the girl already had her plans of modus operandi! We were using a gold Humber Snipe/ Scepter, quite luxurious with highly padded seats, especially at the back. After a while, she insisted on me driving to show her how it should be done, also telling me where I should drive and eventually, stop. She was forward and driven! She told me about her horse and how she loved, riding. Before you could say 'Tally-ho!' she was on top trying to ride me. I nodded to the back seat and was amazed at how deftly she squeezed her ample butt and hips between the front seats and then swivelled her body so that by the time she landed on the back seat, she was not only facing me and dishevelled but ready, with her skirt halfway up her ample and lily-white thighs, with her legs parted. "Oh my!" she said. "What must you think of me?"

"I think you are gorgeous!"

"Really? Well if that's the case, do something!" She had chosen a secluded spot near to Hampstead Heath, so I took a chance. I lifted her butt, got my fingertips under her panties and pulled them off! Ooh! You, naughty boy! She panted. She was gushing like the Rivers of Babylon. She was gyrating for the Full Monty but I was scared. I felt safe in the arms of an older woman but not with this young girl, prostate before me. I felt responsible but I did not want to be. Suddenly, in my mind's eye, I saw my earlier, blond-haired, blue-eyed girl, also prostate before me and again succumbed to the cute essence of her sweet femininity. I felt an aura emanating from her persona of surprise, confusion and exquisite pleasure. After a few more lessons, she was more than capable of reciprocation, rewarding me with financial tips; especially so when she passed her driving test, first time — and her brother did not! He failed his first test for the same reason I did — over confident!

Memories of My Way!
1966

In retrospect, 1966 was a year of transformation for me, from a mature adolescent to an immature young man. I unconsciously lowered the severe discipline which I had imposed upon myself in respect of my work ethic and that, which I thought I should adopt, to please others. Girls seemed to be attracted to me, maybe because of my brand-new Mini Cooper, in which I had them 'cooped up!' It was British Racing Green, with a white top and became my obsession; even during the warranty period I needed a new gear box! I bought her many gifts; leopard skin seat covers, back and front; veneered dashboard; tachometer; combination locked handbrake; lightweight alloy racing mirrors; panoramic mirror; large-bore exhaust pipe down the middle; racing tyres plus various bits and pieces. She was my lover! And I drove her wild. I lost her twice, both on right-hand corners in Cornwall in the summer of '66! The first was driving fast down an inclined hill. You know the kind, high-stoned hills to the right and nothing to the left, apart from a safety barrier.

Colin was with me, both wearing Kangol seat belts, before seat belts were obligatory! I decided on my line through the corner and put the pedal to the metal. As I drove through the corner, the road suddenly dropped away into a reverse camber. I lost adhesion and around we went — one and a half revolutions. I managed to keep on the road without hitting the barrier or going over the side. As we jolted to a halt, albeit facing the other way, my attention was drawn to the interior mirror — a coach was chugging up the hill, on the other side of the road. A few moments later and we could have ended up in the grill — and beyond.

The second incident, a few days later (obviously I did not learn my lesson), occurred when we met up with Brian, of Sun Valley Caravan Park fame, Pentewan Sands, near to Mevagissey. He was the one who, three years before, had the Triumph Vitesse and I, the Ford Escort estate car. He now had a 1800cc souped-up Beetle and I had my Mini Cooper, albeit 998cc. off the factory assembly line. We all decided to go for a drink — fatal! There were three of us in each car. Testosterone was rife! Not a word was mentioned but we all knew what was going to happen. The start flag came down and we were off! Fuck! His car could shift but unbelievably I caught him on the corners. I couldn't pass because were driving along narrow Cornish country lanes. Out of the corner, the Beetle was like 'shit off of a shovel'! The driver was good as well. My concentration level was intense. After thirty minutes or so, we arrived at the pub.

After only an hour or so, we were off again. Although still fast we were following the same pattern; Brian would zoom off and I would catch him at the corners but no opportunity to overtake. I was bored. So, I determined to let him go and then I would catch him up! This meant I could drive through the corners faster — which I loved. After two or three minutes, I put my foot down! I was through the corners like a knife through butter — until... another corner. I took my line and imagined the curvature around the other side. I was flat out, on the limit of adhesion. Suddenly the curve straightened into a bridge! Instinctively I tweaked the steering wheel to straighten but instantaneously lost her. Here we go again — around and around. I recall the smell of rubber and watching skid marks appear in front of me as I fought to control her, and we skidded backwards in a zigzag pattern. I was annoyed with myself. I quickly drove off. After a while I saw Brian, pulled over, waiting for me. "What happened?"

"I stopped for a pee!"

I'll never forget the day I bumped into Socrates! I was stationary, sitting in my Mini Cooper in a side street, off Hampstead Road, south of Mornington Crescent, near to Warren Street. I had given a lift to Colin who was in an appointment, selling a Telstor telephone answering machine; something amazingly I would also do, nine years later, for the same company. Keith, Colin's elder brother, had recently returned to England from New Zealand to whence he had moved, eight years earlier. He was entrepreneurial and had secured the position of agent for Telstor; Colin joined him.

While I was waiting, I was reading a book which I had recently purchased from Reader's Digest. It was entitled *"Great Lives — Great Deeds"* It was a condensation of people and events throughout history that have impacted on the world. It was the great appetiser for the future revelation of my intelligent ignorance! As I scanned through the contents, a chapter caught my eye — "He Taught us how to Think!" My attention was caught. I turned back to the page and there was a coloured drawing of Socrates' bust with an impish smile, a large domed forehead, little hair on his head but plenty on his face. As I began to read, I was mesmerized by the character of Socrates; his boundless energy in search of the truth by employing logical thinking. His audacious questioning of authority to establish reason behind its laws and war. His endeavour to define intrinsic values and re-evaluate beliefs that were based on superstition and not logic/fact. His humble approach of first stating that he was a man of little education and did not know the answer to any given question but was merely endeavouring to find an answer through debate. This clever approach gave tremendous advantage to Socrates in that his adversary was enveloped in a false sense of security, feeling confident to reveal his true opinion, albeit self-opinionated and invariably based on pre-judgments.

As an example, an army recruitment office would stand on a boulder in Athens and encourage young men to join the army with his patriotic rhetoric.

Army Officer: "Have the courage to fight and die for the glory of Athens!"

Socrates: "Pardon my intrusion but what do you mean by courage?"

Army Officer: "Courage is sticking to your post and not retiring, when there is danger."

Socrates: "But supposing good strategy shows that it would be better to retreat and take up a better defensive position. Would that be cowardice?"

Army Officer: "Of course not!"

Socrates: "Then courage is not sticking to your post or perhaps retreating, is it? What would you say courage is?"

Army Officer: "I'm baffled. I don't exactly know."

Socrates: "I don't know either. But I wonder if it is nothing more than keeping our presence of mind to do that which is right, irrespective of danger, ridicule or criticism?"

This way of thinking changed my life — FOREVER!

Memories of My way!
Summer 1966

This new knowledge was agitating and exciting my latest mental creative energy. I was brimming with the desire to learn more and more — and more! To learn more and more, about what? I did not know! All I did know was that I wanted — nay, needed a new challenge! I wanted adventure! Then, bingo! I had the answer. The one thing that clarified my searching mind. The one challenge that was big enough to satisfy and calm my restless energy — NEW ZEALAND! Go to New Zealand! It was the answer to everything. I knew I could get a job there — I was a bricklayer by trade, albeit a salesman by profession. Every time I thought of it, I was consumed with excitement! I was obsessed; I could not stop thinking about it. Colin was obviously up for It- his brother Keith was already there. Then we sold the idea to the other two friends, Brian and Gilbert. At that time, Colin and I were twenty-two, Brian twenty-one and Gilbert twenty. We had all attended the same school, our beloved Acland Boys Central School, Fortess Road, London, MW5, between Tufnell Park and Kentish

Town. Colin, Brian and I had played football together for the Old Boys team in Belgium, Holland and Spain. Gilbert had been the captain of the Young Old Boys team, when I broke my collarbone.

I got everything organized with the travelling arrangements. It was going to take six months to save enough money for travel expenses and pocket money when we arrived in NZ. We were to go by boat via Caracas, South America, then across the Pacific Ocean all the way down to New Zealand. The complete voyage would take six weeks! I was euphoric. The power and intensity of my enthusiasm took me into a new, strange and unreal world. I was high on adrenalin. I concluded that I needed more money, so I decided to be a part-time mini-cab driver. However, I could not do that with my current girl — my beloved Mini Cooper. So, guess what I did? I chopped her in for a MKII Ford Consul 1700cc.

OMG! What have I done? The fulfilment of my dream knew no boundaries. I was obsessed!

But a dream was all it remained; it never came to fruition. It brought my mother to the edge of a nervous breakdown!

During the summer of 1966, Colin and I vacationed in Felixstowe on the East Coast, where his parents had a caravan. We drove there in my Consul and later in the day met up with Brian and Gil. In the evening we went bar-hopping. In the last bar, I saw this mature girl looking at me from a distance, so I beckoned her over to where I was sitting; she came. She was bold, older than me with sex oozing from every pore of her persona. I beckoned her, and she came across me. She explained that she was leaving soon to take her company home but if I was interested, she would come back for me. Colin, Brian and Gil left and I duly waited. She soon returned in a new Vauxhall Viva and opened the door for me. As I sat down and closed the door, I could sense the determination of this lady — to fuck me! She drove off to a secluded spot overlooking the North Sea. She came on to me immediately, with both boobs blasting. After a short bout of foreplay in the front seats, she scrambled onto the backseats, pulling on my wrist. Before I could say, Jack Robinson, she was on top of me, going hell for leather! I think she was disappointed with my non-performance. Well, c'mon, I'm only human, twenty-two and never been fucked before. I had previously been the dominant partner. This was a new experience for me — but I wasn't complaining. Doing sex in a small two-door car is not to be recommended, especially if your partner is of a demonstrative nature. When I had recovered (which wasn't long in those far off distant days), I determined to give her 'what for!' Somehow, I managed to get her off of me and then me onto her. It wasn't exactly romantic but she didn't want romance anyway. What she wanted was raw, basic, rough sex. Well, she got it and the outcome was 'ginormous'. I managed to last longer, long enough for her to hit the roof of the diminutive Vauxhall Viva, which wasn't that far away. She became a wild cat, more and more greedy for continuous gratification, constantly protecting myself from her wild gesticulations and ginormous outcomes. I lay prostate, 'cream-crackered' as a result of my exhausted energy. As we were tidying up, my genitals became the recipient of an amazing gesture of gratitude. What's the point of going to the 'seaside' if you don't share your 'stick of rock'? Lick, lick!

When I returned to London, I was approached to play for a local football team in Hornsey Rise, Realm. This was a local pub team of local Jack the Lads; some of whom I knew from primary school. Some blew close to the parameters of the law but had likeable and showman-like personalities. Two attracted me to play for the team, Frankie Harris and Kenny Taylor. These two players were heroes of mine at my primary school and older than I. I recall an illuminating account of their football prowess being read out in school assembly on one occasion for winning an important football trophy for Duncombe Road School, N19, and here I was, about to play with them. They put me in at centre forward. At 5'7" I was not the tallest centre forward in the world but I was fast, off the spot, I had vision, hard-kicker, versatile and strong! A previous team that I had played for, Wessex, out of Holloway Road, in 1959–60, dubbed me the 'Steam Roller'. The name was actually coined by Jack, a previous Scottish International footballer who acted as scout for the team. He actually came down by bus, to Holmes Road, Kentish Town, Working Man's Club, where I was weight training at the tender age of fifteen, to sign me up! He had previously been to my house in 42, Calverly Grove N19, to sign me up, but Mum told him where I was, and down he came to Kentish Town and signed me up, there and then!

Memories of My Way!
Summer/Autumn 1966

So, I played for Realm but didn't really enjoy it. I scored goals, top-scorer; even one from a corner kick but I was not enjoying football. There was no discipline in the team, especially in defence. I recall in one match I had scored two goals, but we still lost 2-3, when Frankie Harris said, "How does it feel scoring two goals and being on the losing side?" I had no answer but suddenly realized at that point, that I was wasting my time with Realm. And, I admit I was enjoying my super sex-gig in Felixstowe with the Crazy Lady. But looming on the horizon, was the life-long, psychological ball and chain I had had to bear, all of my life, about to become stronger! Although I had no control over being an only child! Although Mum was coping with me now living in London and her still living in Aylesbury with Dad, the news of the prospect of me emigrating to New Zealand was sending her into spasms of depression. Her constant pleading with me not to go was taking a toll on my conscience. Eventually I plucked up the courage to tell, Brian, Colin and Gilbert, that I was not going to NZ. I managed to get the money back, deposited with the travel agents, minus 10% which I nobly paid out of my own pocket.

During 1966 I had stopped being a driving instructor for BSM and went back to being an insurance agent with London and Manchester. This time I was working out of the Finsbury Park office and not the Highgate office, B16 — albeit still out of the 'B' Divisional office in Seven Sisters Road, opposite Finsbury Park — but it was never the same. I had changed big time. I was SO restless. I wanted new challenges and adventure but did not know how to go about it within the psychological constraints of my mother's influence.

To quell my torment, I worked — more! In addition to my income as an insurance agent, I was also part-time mini-cabbing. Then, by chance, I crossed the threshold of a shop in Hornsey Road, N19, just around the corner from Corbyn Street (where Ronnie Poole used to live; one of the seven who went to ACLAND from Duncombe Road School in 1955) and there, lo and behold, I saw and recalled an Acland Old Boy who was the owner of the shop — John. He was selling — you name it, at discount prices. John was buying from wholesalers from Highbury Corner, Islington and East London, who in turn, were buying in inexpensive items from overseas, then selling retail out of the shop. When I told him I was an insurance agent with 400 clients he offered me a proposition on a sale or return basis. I took him up on his offer and from out of the back of the Ford Consul I was selling watches, cufflinks, various items of jewellery, woollen blankets, clocks, a variety of goods. I set up agents to sell for me; I was earning good money. Ironically, the front downstairs room at 42, Calverly Grove, where

Mum, Dad and I had lived from 1958-January 1965, was the storeroom. I was earning good money.

It was during this period of 1966 that I met Eddie Clarke. He was an existing client of L&M Assurance Co. Ltd. He had a refurbished flat in a largish terraced house in Osbalderston Road, London, N16; a predominantly Jewish area of Stamford Hill. I called at his address to collect his life assurance premiums. On Eddie opening the front door, I quickly introduced myself and stepped into the large hall. As the door closed behind me, I noticed a guitar leaning against the wall. I said, "Is that your guitar?"

He said, "Yes! I play and sing — Country & Western!" Bingo!

Eddie and I struck up a friendship and began to meet at his place, to jam. He would play rhythm guitar and sing Country & Western. I would sing popular songs to which he would accompany; we soon started talking about starting a group. I said, "I know someone who can play bass-guitar!" Colin; we all met up. Then Colin introduced a lead guitarist and then a drummer popped up from somewhere and suddenly, we had a group. The only instrument I could play was the vocal cords! Soon we got a gig at The Rink, Finsbury Park on the corner of Seven Sisters Road and Stroud Green Road, N4. Originally an ice rink, then a cinema, now a large hall for bingo and various social gatherings.

The group kicked-off with dreary Hank Williams' songs, with Eddie singing (Eddie was a depressive type), boring the audience to distraction. Then on comes I with two bright and breezy songs; "*The Young Ones*" and "*Bachelor Boy*", both hits by Cliff Richard (was it the Webb in Harry that saved Richard from the Cliff?) The audience burst into a cauldron of energy, appreciation and applause. But guess what? Thereafter, I was out of the group; I had inadvertently upstaged Eddie.

I was still with L&M and selling goods out of the boot of my MKII Consul around Stamford Hill and earning good pocket money, especially as Christmas approached. However, I was still so insatiably restless and for some inexplicable reason, commenced at 5:00 am on the 1st January 1967 as a milkman!

OMG! What am I doing? As part of the milk round were lift-less flats (no elevators). Right! Get a crate, refer to the order book, and put the bottles of milk in the spaces, as many orders as I could carry. One gold top, two white; one white; two gold; one white, two sterilised, two pots of cream, etc., etc. Then after climbing six flights of stairs and reaching the first doorstep to drop off, the front door opens. "Good morning, dear! Can I have two extra pints, please?"

I stuck it for a few weeks but then back to a more leisurely life, driving London Transport buses.

Memories of My Way!
Spring 1967

After joining London Transport and becoming a bus driver, I decided to trade-in my MKII Consul for a British Racing Green MG 1100cc, four-door saloon and do more mini-cabbing between shifts and days off. Then one day, as I was driving along Tottenham High Road, along the one-way system, up from Tottenham Hale, I saw this magnificent black creature; it was an M.G. (Morris Garages) Midget 1100cc, with soft AND Bermuda tops. I had to have her! And have her, I did! After running my fingertips along her silky contours, adjusting her two tops, soft and hard, playing with her control box, she was mine!

You know, tidying up paperwork in 1967 was so simple, straightforward and fast. To qualify for a loan all you had to do was not appear on a blacklist. Now, in this era of computers and computerised people, it takes forever! Furthermore, guess what — I have no credit rating! Why? Because I have not borrowed money for years! I'm not a bad boy, I'm not a good boy; I just don't exist, on computer records!

I remember the salesman to be smart, charming and articulate. On asking him about the acceleration of the Midget he responded, "I believe it is quite vivid!" This was to be the one and only sports car that I would purchase. After a couple of days, I took it back to the dealer and said, "This car doesn't feel as though it is moving."

"That, sir, is because you are so close to the ground." He was right. I could take her flat out and still feel as though I was sitting in the front room. On one occasion I took her up to Silverstone for a good thrashing. At the end of the day I had worn out a set of tyres. Someone had a stopwatch and I was soon making quick times around the club circuit, especially for a factory-built vehicle. So much so that I decided to write to Stirling Moss about the times. He was courteous enough to reply (I still have the letter to this day, 49 years later) and he referred me to the Racing Stables at Brands Hatch (to follow).

Tring, in Hertfordshire, had resounded three times in my life!

1. I was evacuated to Tring, when the V-2 rockets were falling on London in 1944 WWII.

2. I was a Country Bus and Green Line coach driver out of Tring bus terminal.

3. Stirling Moss had lived and learned to drive in Tring on his father's farm, when he was a boy.

However, as I would soon learn in January/February of 1968, the slower a car feels, the faster it goes but the safety margins are reduced!

When Jim Clark, Formula 1 Racing Driver and World Champion in 1963 and 1965 was killed on 7th April 1968 (two days after my twenty-fourth birthday), my days of fast driving reduced a few miles per hour.

Memories of My Way!
1967

After two short uneventful episodes as first a milkman and then a bread salesman, selling out of the back of a Hovis van in Cambridgeshire, I decided that I wanted the challenge of driving buses; double-decker buses in London. I applied at the Walthamstow, London Red Bus Depot, Hoe Street E17; located on a bend. As I recall the training was at Chiswick West London. I did the bit, the full monty skid patch 'n' all! Quite scary really. I was asked by the instructor standing next to me in the bus to drive at speed, towards a brick wall. We drove, closer and closer — and closer. Then suddenly the instructor yells, "Handbrake!" I racked up the large contraption, positioned to my left and immediately we are into a spin of epic proportions around and around on the deliberately wet and slippery surface. Eventually the bus stops and rock 'n' rolls from side to side but NOT the base, the base remains as solid as a rock with the four wheels firmly stuck to the ground.

After passing the driving test, first time, to obtain my PSV

License, Passenger Service Vehicle License (which meant I could drive up to 52-seater coaches and get paid for the experience), I chose to work out of the Wood Green bus terminal, London N8. My reasoning for this was to experience more driving in less congested areas. My main route was the number 29 route from South Mimms in South Hertfordshire to Victoria Station in West London. Matt Monroe was a conductor on the number 14 bus route from Hornsey Rise London N19 to Pimlico in South West London. The number 14 bus turned in Sunnyside Road just before the rise/hill of Hornsey Rise. Where the bus stopped in Sunnyside Road was the *Favourite* pub where Matt (Terry?) Monroe was discovered.

At this time, Mum decided she wanted to move back to London — to a council flat in Clapton, London E5. It was a disaster and very soon we all decided to put in for another council transfer, back to Aylesbury — OMG! But we got lucky,

quite soon with a single lady, originally from London who detested Aylesbury and wanted back to East London ASAP!

So, around the summer of '67 we all moved back to Aylesbury; to a two-bedroomed semi-detached house in Coventon Road. It was a pleasant enough area with a school, small shopping area and with us, situated opposite a small church. I was transferred from London Red Buses in Wood Green, North London to Country Green Buses in Tring, Hertfordshire, ironically to where I had been evacuated in 1944/ 45. My conductor colleague was a Londoner; a big man in his fifties, red-faced with a full head of white hair. He had recently moved from London to Tring, to retire in a few years' time. His son, also big, was already working out of the Tring bus terminal as a mechanic. So, my conductor was, "As happy as a sandboy!"

Driving through Berko (Berkhamstead) High Street on one occasion, I stopped at a white compulsory bus stop to take on passengers. In the queue was a young blond stunner; tall, good figure and coyly smiling in my direction. My body quickly told me that I wanted her! But how? As I drove off, conscious of her seated behind me somewhere in the bus, I contrived of an ingenious idea. That night I would write a polite note of introduction charm and persuade her, via my words telling her how beautiful I thought she was and how much I would (love to get inside her knickers) love to meet her and hoped that we could be meaningful friends. My conductor colleague agreed to be 'postman' and pass over the note to the golden damsel. Apparently, she was a little embarrassed but followed through with a reciprocal note. The following day she succumbed to my words and agreed to meet. We went for a ride on Black Beauty; she liked my Bermuda hard-top and remarked on its virility, more than once. She said, "Can we open her up and give her a good thrashing? I'm SO excited!" So we drove straight back to her place! She was nineteen, with a great body, and legs up to her arm-pits. Her lily-white thighs seemed to go on forever and so it took a long while to slowly pass my fingertips along the soft flesh, just before the welcoming destination. The surface had become wet and slippery and difficult for them (fingertips) to stay upright, so they slipped over into their destination in that position. Of course, I took her on a few 'flights' via Air Lingus for which she was most grateful before banging her, hard and deep — and she was deep!

She evolved to be somewhat of a snob, methinks, fuelled by her well-to-do mother who wanted something more sophisticated than I, for her daughter. Also, no husband/dick. Didn't think of it at the time but now believe that a threesome was well on the card.

Also, at that time, I was well into drawing and colouring and developed an emotional affinity with the paintings of Van Gogh. I copied the self-portrait of Van Gogh with the bandage covering the remainder of his right ear, which he cut off and gave to a prostitute. I sent the picture to the girl — I never saw her again, even at the bus stop! Perhaps she thought I was going to give her my right ear!

Memories of My Way — And the '60s! February 1968

Albeit, still in a long-term quandary as to my future, I was still addicted to driving cars very quickly and over the limit wherever the opportunity presented itself; I LOVED the adrenalin rush when hanging on by the seat of my pants! During some part of February, I was 'riding' my Black Beauty, my MG (Morris Garages) Midget 1100cc. (1.1 horsepower) to Aylesbury from the Tring Country bus terminal. I had just completed my Green Line Coach route from Tring, Hertfordshire, up to Aylesbury, Bucks, where I was living at the time. Then, turn around and drive back down the A41 (old road), down to Watford, through London and on to Colliers Wood, in East Sussex. Take a rest, then back on the road, all the way back to Tring.

So here I am, having finished my route, leaving Tring bus terminal, driving back to Aylesbury via Aston Clinton at about 6.00 pm. It was pitch black and cold with humps of packed ice stacked along the middle of the two-way road. The street lights were on and sparkling against the back-drop of the black sky.

The speed of the traffic was tediously slow, seemingly slower, as my patience grew faster and faster. I drove through Aston Clinton and eventually approached the long straight stretch of road leading to Aylesbury.

I suddenly saw a gap in the ice and before I knew it, I was on the other side of the road with nothing coming the other way, just faint lights in the far-off distance. I carefully accelerated (as I felt the slippery surface close to the skin of my butt, albeit just a few inches below) past the line of vehicles, causing the hold up and my impatience, to fester. Eventually I was alongside the culprit of the intolerably slow speed. It was one of those old, old pickup trucks, seemingly fuelled by steam, which were still around in the 60s. I passed this antiquated piece of combustion with ease. However, the new challenge was, how to get back over, onto the correct side of the road, especially when the centralized hill of ice was higher! As I tried to return to the correct lane, for some reason momentum was throwing me back onto the wrong side of the road. Furthermore, the lights that were faint were now brighter and larger! I swung the MG to the left in the hope that this time, it would get over the hump of ice, but it threw me back again. The situation was now becoming

critical Through the darkness I could see a blur of lights, three feet off the ground, seven feet off the ground, twelve feeet off the ground. The blur emerged as a double-decker country bus! OMG! There was just enough time and space for one more attempt to mount the hump of ice and get over onto the correct side of the road.

This time I decided to take more of an acute angle so there

would be less lateral resistance of the packed ice against the underside of the car, then accelerate as Black Beauty would rise and straddle the hump. This proved to be disastrous! The dynamics were unpredictable, I lost control of the car, which inexplicably was now careering to the right, towards the bus. The front wheels of the Midget were locked hard left but Black Beauty was sliding, at speed, to the right, out of control! Did my life flash before me? NO! I was real, adjusting my body to resist going through the screen. BANG! I hit the double-decker bus but fortunately not head on. I hit the large, exposed, black mudguard. Then, and fortunately again due to the fortuitous angle of 'Beauty' at the point of impact, plus the fact that the front wheels were hard locked to the left and no road surface resistance, providence determined that momentum would change direction to the left! I smashed through the packed ice along the middle of the road, ending up in the gutter, on the other side of the road. I was alive — and — uninjured but Black Beauty had been severely hurt and was close to being 'put down'! The bus couldn't move; the black mudguard was imbedded in the front, offside right tyre!

How embarrassing is this?

"Country Buses Bus Driver smashes his private car into a Country Bus, causing it to be taken out of operation. He tells his story, sitting in the damaged bus whilst still in his Country Bus uniform, waiting for a bus to pick him up." I was twenty-three!

Memories of My Way!
Summer of '68

After working with London Transport for thirteen months driving London Red Buses, Country Buses then culminating in being appointed a driver of the 'exclusive' Green Line Buses, I decided that enough was enough! I decided to open up my PSV (Passenger Service Vehicles) license 'key' of opportunity and work, full time for a coach company out of Hemel Hempstead in Hertfordshire by the name of 'Ronsway'. The company had a variety of coaches, including 52-seaters. I didn't work there for long; I was there to drive, not to clean up mess! However, I do remember one incident which was a breakthrough experience.

I recall driving employees from a company out of a business park in Hemel to an event in Birmingham. On the journey one of the younger fellows, Tim, of similar age as I, twenty-three, engaged in conversation (primarily at his surprise of my ability to drive a 52-seater coach at such a young age); so much so that after we had all checked into the hotel in Birmingham, Tim and I decided to drive back into

Central Birmingham in the 52-seater! We parked- somewhere and ended up in a disco. For a year or so I had been admiring the curvaceous bodies of the young black girls coming over to England from various islands of the West Indies (as named by Christopher Columbus). I was attracted to their large 'come to bed' eyes and smiling faces, their friendly natures, sparkling teeth, full kissable lips and gorgeous butts! Then suddenly, in the disco — amazingly, there, before me, were two such beautiful creatures. OMG! My heart was pounding — I could hear it! My breath stopped — I couldn't breathe!

Especially one specimen of feminine beauty was of immense attraction to me. "She was the cutest thing you ever did see!" And guess what? They were both looking over at Tim and I, giggling. OMG! "I've gotta have her! I've gotta have her! I've got to HAVE HER!" I nudged Tim; he was also ogling. I looked at him and nodded, he nodded back. Within seconds we had split the girls on the dance floor and they were now, willingly, in our arms. I could NOT resist, immediately, placing my lips on those of Clarisse. The sensation was amazing and unforgettable. I had never experienced such a feeling. An envelopment of soft yet firm caressing flesh exuding subliminal eroticism and promise. The outcome for me was a massive, throbbing erection and I let Clarisse know it. She said, "Oh MY! Naughty boy!"

"Because of you," I whispered.

"Why me?" she coyly asked.

"Because you are absolutely GORGEOUS!" I responded, breathlessly.

"And you are so handsome," she whispered, close to my

ear. We were locked in each other's arms. Tim was doing great as well. I explained the situation to Clarisse about the coach. She was up for it and so was the other girl. So, back to the 52-seater, we ran! I claimed the back seat — fantastic! Clarisse could not wait! It transpired that both girls were trainee nurses and were adept at removing patients clothing and well versed in the human anatomy. I was about to enjoy those training skills! Suddenly my trousers and underpants were on the coach floor alongside Clarisse, who was on her knees before me, fondling my penis with such delicacy, erotic precision and visual curiosity; she could see it in the darkness. OMG! Was I about to experience the unbelievable? Yes! I was! Even now, nearly 50 years later I still cannot, fully express, in words, or give literal credibility to the exquisite sensations pulsating through my body when the lips of Clarisse encompassed my penis. I recall gasping, a hollowness in my stomach and an overall sensation, as if I were floating in the air. The continuation of her facial orifice was, "seemingly" endless! I was so quick!

Clarisse did not bother looking around for external means of tidying up the outcome; she had already done that, internally, in a natural way. When, eventually, she was able to speak, she said, in a hoarse and sultry voice, "You are a long boy!" And then, before our very eyes, there he was again — ready, willing and able! With that sight in the eyes and face of Clarisse, up went her dress and down come her panties, then 'up and over' as she quickly straddled my lower torso. Soon I was totally and utterly inside her, "Knockin' on Heaven's (back) door!" Outside, I was "Ringing her Bell", with my teasing fingertips. Clarisse moaned and groaned as she was caught in a spasm of continuous grinding movements against my enlarged penis, culminating in orgasm after orgasm.

Eventually she slid off me, panting, heavily. Now it was my turn. I rearranged our positions. Clarisse was now under me! As our genitals touched, again there was already an open invitation, waiting for me. The entrance was smooth and encouraging without interruption. My member was like a rod of pre-stressed steel — it never bent or faltered. Clarisse couldn't "Adam & Eve" it! And so, I gave her more! Oh Bernie! Oh Bernie! Oh Bernie! Again, tumultuous orgasms. We took a breather but no withdrawal. And here we go again. This one would be the best one for Clarisse. I rearranged the position of her body on the bench seat for deep penetration and muscular leverage. This time I knew I would last longer and control, to some extent, my excitement. I moved Clarisse up against the side of the coach as a 'back-stop!' I threw her legs onto my shoulders and just fell inside of her, as far as nature would allow. Her eyes popped and her mouth dropped open; my tongue quickly fell, deep inside! One orifice to go…

Memories of 'MY WAY' (Spring of '68)

I had been talking to Rob Smith, the cheeky cockney bricklayer, living across the road, with his young and pretty wife and three kids in Cannock Road, Aylesbury. As a quick aside. A few years later, after I moved back to North London and Mum and Dad had moved back to Coventon Road in Aylesbury, Rob did a smart move. His wife had run off with the husband of the next-door neighbours, leaving Rob holding the three babies. As invariably happens, the new-flung infatuation became deflated. Rob took her back but then quickly and summarily, left her — holding the three babies, herself!

So back to the story; Rob had won a contract as the 'bricklayer subbie' (sub-contractor) for a new housing estate in 'Berko', Berkhamsted, Herts, just north of Watford. He was building up a gang of brickies and hod-carriers and asked me to join because he knew I had been a bricklayer. However, I hadn't laid a brick, only chicks, since August 1963; it was now May '68. Furthermore, I had previously and solely ever worked on big sites, somewhat protected from the elements. This was a raw, open site, high on hills overlooking Berkhamsted; it was bleak and unwelcoming. Plus, I did not like the attitude of the workers, callous, piss-taking ignoramuses — and NOT tradesman. I decided to stick it for a few months — why? Couldn't tell you, exactly. Forever challenging and competing with myself. I had, I thought, become a little 'soft' and I wanted to prove to myself that I could overcome the pain and torment of the work, the workers and the ambiance, of the building trade, again. Then, after a few months, when I had satisfied myself that I had, in fact, proven myself to myself — I quit! Rob was upset but I wanted out! Furthermore, the winter was drawing in and I determined that working on hilltops, overlooking Berko, with the cold and wind blustering around, was not the most sensible place to be.

Dad had got himself holed up for the winter, working on the new Aylesbury Town Centre; it was big. Dad spoke to the foreman on my behalf. So, I left the hills of Berko, and made a start at the new Aylesbury Town Centre as a bricklayer.

Straightaway, the foreman, of the old, old school, put me to task. He thought that I was a chancer, never served my time as an apprentice, which I hadn't as expressed in a previous chapter, but he was not aware of my 'do or die' attitude, or my knowledge of the building trade, especially bricklaying; I just LOVE proving people wrong!

First job was to build a chimney with fire resistant bricks, an unusual chore for ANY bricklayer because the process of laying is completely different from that of laying conventional bricks. The bricks are much lighter in weight and dipped into a fire-resistant liquid mixed with cement; how many chimneys were there around anyway, even in 1968? But fortunately, I had had the previous experience of laying these kinds of bricks when working with my Uncle Fred at the police cadet college, Sunbury-on-Thames, in 1962–63. So Mr 'Clever Dick' Foreman did not catch me out; in fact, he was astonished at my ability to cope with the unusual chore!

However, not satisfied, he then put me to task again! He got me to build a dump-chute. This was on the ground level of the area to be used by future market traders in the market place of the new town centre. The structure, therefore, needed to be strong; there were red semi-engineering bricks to be laid. The texture of these bricks is the complete opposite to the firebricks. The firebricks are light and porous; by contrast, the engineering bricks are heavy and non-porous. Furthermore, the common fletton brick was also to be used and, at some places in the overall brickwork, the two varying bricks to be bonded together. The challenge with that was, engineering bricks are generally larger than flettons. So, I needed to work the overall measurements to the size engineering bricks and make up the difference in the fletton bed-joint, with mortar. If I had chosen the flettons to work to, then the engineering bricks would have been too large to fit into the toothing of the flettons! That's what the foreman was banking on, so that, at a certain stage, the whole structure would not be feasible to complete! He could then humiliate me and even sack me!

Furthermore, on alternate courses of the reds, 3three-inchwire mesh was to be laid in the mortar bed-joint! The effect of this was to make the bed-joint of that course, even larger. The purpose, to make the wall stronger against the battering it would subsequently receive from careless market traders.

The biggest challenge of all, however, was the confined space in which to work, due to the overall size of the concrete bunker itself. It was about five feet high, four feet wide, three feet deep. Where to start was the key to not building oneself in! Like solitaire where the idea is to end up with one peg in the middle hole. If I didn't start in the right place, then I would not be able to have the reach/room to finish. I started at the back, right-hand corner and 'racked and toothed' my way out! I could finish solitaire, with the last peg in the middle hole, when I was nine years of age. I'll never forget the look on the foreman's face when he returned the next day, when I had finished the job! He just grunted with a nod of the head!

Memories of My Way!

(Christmas '68 / summer of '69/ New Year 1969 Christmas was coming and I needed MORE money, so I rented a stall in the New Aylesbury market for the last Friday and Saturday before Christmas. The previous weekend I had driven down to Hornsey Rise, the area in North London where I had been brought up. I drove to John's shop, my friend from Acland Boys School in Hornsey Road. Hornsey Road eventually crosses Seven Sisters Road, whereby if one was driving from north to south, one would turn left along Seven Sisters Road and eventually arrive in the Finsbury Park district, just past The Astoria Picture Palace, where this story began on the 11th November 1959. Then around the one-way system and into St. Thomas' Road, where Dad was born and bred, and on to the original Arsenal Football Stadium, to where the team had transferred from Woolwich Arsenal (south of the River Thames) in the early twentieth Century.

    I had earned good money working with John in '67, when I had returned to L&M Ass. Co. Ltd. as an insurance agent. So, as I was in good stead with him, he let me have a lot of gear on a sale or return basis. I took blankets, ornaments, household goods, Christmas stuff — trees, toys, gifts, also cufflinks, watches, all and sundry and carted it all back to Aylesbury, in readiness to set up my stall on Friday morning. It felt ironic that I was setting up as a market trader on the site where I was also working as a bricklayer, albeit hoarded and boarded off from the public. The inevitable happened. Tom, the bricklayer foreman, saw me but did not say anything. However, when I returned to work on the Monday, he did say something. I said, "Ok! Stop my money for the day!" He did not. I had a feeling that he secretly admired my entrepreneurial attitude to earn more money.

Christmas came and went, as usual, totally boring for me; virtually the same with the first half of '69. As summer approached, I had taken to walking to work with a cut-down pair of jeans with just socks and Dr. Marten boots, my torso revealed to the early morning sun. This was extremely unusual in 1969. Every time I did this, I had astounded gazes from all and sundry. Being a frustrated entertainer, I loved it! Although I must admit, I did have a great physique in 1969, especially after a year back in the building trade (later to be called the construction industry) — now approaching the age of twenty-five.

I was also working out and attending an extreme fitness class in the evenings, which on more than one occasion had brought me to the point of vomiting! Those fellas WERE — FIT, many of whom were rugby players. However, when it came to basketball, I had them by the short and curlies! I am naturally a great dribbler with a basketball but not a football.

It was during those basketball matches that I first heard the word 'mesmerizing!' The coach, who was a professional rugby player and unbelievably fit, always leading by example, coined the term regarding my dribbling prowess. He said, "You are mesmerizing them." He was one of those university types, with a posh accent but enormous commitment and follow through. I had/have very quick reflexes and hands. Also, the agility to change pace, balance and direction instantaneously. The ball appears to stick to my hand but I could never do it with my feet, don't know why. I think because I love to kick the ball with precise accuracy.

"Well, here comes summer…" My good friend Brian had booked us a package holiday in Majorca, Spain and at age twenty-five, this was my first time to fly! I loved it but was somewhat perturbed when I couldn't find my parachute! In my ignorance I honestly believed that every passenger was issued with a parachute, in the event of the plane crashing. It was at that moment I reconciled myself, as I had done in 1955 when I was about to take my 11+ entrance examination that, "Why worry; worry gets you nowhere at all!" I adopted the mindset that, what can I do about it? Nothing! That chosen mindset put me in good stead in that, ever since July 1969, whenever I walk into a plane, a sense of serenity envelopes me to the extent that I am invariably asleep by the time the plane is taking off.

As soon as I emerged from the plane, I felt the shock of the hot climate on my face; like walking into an oven. Sure, I had been to Spain in 1963 to play football but that time we travelled by ship and train so the climate change was gradual. This time — wow! Brian had done a good job! Good flight from Gatwick; train to Gatwick, during which time Brian was eulogising all the way about a girl at work with whom he had fallen in love (infatuation). Having said that, he did subsequently marry her and still is married to her (Brian always did submit himself to female domination). What some men will do when they are not confident about 'tasting' — pussy!

So, we have arrived! What to do now la? Eating food that gave me the runs! (Body not used to the oil). Drinking copious amounts of Cuba Libre (Bacardi and Coke). Swimming; always swim the first length underwater to gain attention! I won a competition singing Delilah! We got friendly with two Dutch girls. "No sex please, we're British!" I tried water skiing for the first time and as you can imagine, I took to it "like a fish/duck takes to water!" Well I AM athletic — right? At the end of the session, as the boat swung into shore and off again for the last time, I let go of the horizontal bar on the towing rope and skied, hands held high, towards the beach, slowly coming to a halt just before the dry sand; then I fell over because I couldn't slip out of the ski shoes! A few moments later I saw George Best, with his entourage, drinking outside a bar on the beach. He didn't seem to recognise me!

There were no great highs or lows in Majorca for Brian or I, except that it caused a change of scenery which, as usual, had the effect of making me discontented when I returned to good ol' Blighty! The return to England for Brian was THE major turning point in his life to date. He put his eulogising into action.

Memories of My Way! (Summer '69)

So, back in England, on the plane without a parachute, from Gatwick to London on the train then back to the Aylesbury by bus public transport. I had a car but no insurance but can't remember why not, I had previously transacted a straight swap with my black mistress for a young white favourite of mine; my MG Midget, Bermuda top on all for an almost new Mini 1000 cc. A young fella in the Aylesbury area had responded to an advert I had placed on postcards in shop windows. He immediately fell in love with my black beauty and wanted her! Even though she had dodgy teeth due to tasteless innovation I had fixed at the front to replace the original grill, lost in the episode of crashing into the offside bumper of a Country Bus. There was not enough money left in Savundra's Insurance Company to buy a new one but the young fella didn't care, nor did Savundra, until he met David Frost on a TV interview!

Back on the site, working on the new Aylesbury Town Centre was boring. The same emotions perpetrated through my persona as in the summer of '63 when I returned to the Ronson site. I was restless — big time!

Furthermore, an excessive amount of testosterone was being manufactured between Dad and myself. I HAD to go! This time I could not afford to consider the emotional overtones of — Mother! I'm out of here! I left Aylesbury for London in August 1969 with GBP 8.00 in my pocket. I plumped for Muswell Hill, London N10 I'll never forget it — it was a Saturday and I needed accommodation — NOW! I called on a letting agent and was given two options. The first one — nothing! And remember, I'm on 'shanks pony' getting around Muswell Hill. Second one, 48, Leaside Avenue, N10, the last house on the left-hand side. A good size, end of terraced Edwardian house. I knocked and a buxom lady opened the front door. Imagine, I had just returned from sunning myself in Majorca and was already well tanned before I left, exposing my body along the roads of Aylesbury as I walked to work. So, I was as brown as a berry! As I walked into the hallway the lady said, "Are you English?"

I said, "Yes! Are you?"

She said, "No! I'm Irish!" (Begorrah!)

I took the room at GBP 4.00 per week and duly paid the first week, upfront! I now had GBP 4.00 left in my pocket! I needed quick money, quick, so I took to knocking on shop doors in Muswell Hill and Palmers Green N13.

As ALWAYS, with committed persistence, I got lucky. I called on a small driving school in Green Lanes, just south of the North Circular Road, which, diagonally north east, on the corner plot, was a great pub named the Cock. It was where Len and I (the man who taught me to drive) sometimes stopped off for a beer or two when out on a lesson.

"No full time — but spare time."

"I'll take it!"

But guess what? I got the full time use of the instruction car; dual controls an' all! Suddenly, I was free!

I recall, in particular, that I had to pick up a Mrs XYZ from her house in Palmerstone Road N13. I imagined a middle-aged female but what emerged through the front door was a small goddess with long blond hair and this time — a Scots accent. It was lust at first sight! She was a little younger than I, cute and oozing sex appeal with a short skirt up to her armpits! I found myself magnetized to glimpsing at her sumptuous half diamond-shaped white panties peeping below her tight skirt. But she was married.

"What is your husband's work?" I probed.

"He is the leader of the XYZ band!" (Quite well known at the time.) (No kids!)

"Don't' you get lonely in that big house?" I enquired.

"I do," she said. After the lesson you can come back for a 'cup of tea', if you want to?"

"But what about your husband?"

"He's on tour in Europe."

"Really; for how long?"

"Another three weeks."

Well, before I could ask her, "What do Scotsman wear under their kilts?" we were in the house frantically pulling off each other's clothes. She grabbed my hand and we rushed upstairs to the large bed. Agnes' skin was like cream; mine? Like coffee. We 'stirred', again and again and again! Agnes, hot, wet and willing, submissive and experienced; she knew what she was doing and what she wanted. She was petite, adjustable and pliable; I think she fell in love with my tanned and taut body and commenced to explore every inch of it, back as well as front. We continued our clandestine affair 'til her husband returned and thereafter when he was off on tour again,

During that period of part-time driving instruction, every morning I would buy an *Evening Standard* newspaper, scanning the jobs ad. section. I had determined that I wanted back in sales! Between lessons, both driving and riding with

Agnes, I would attend interviews but without initial success. Then at last, I was accepted by a film/record company as a salesman, selling records out of the back of a new Ford Transit van, kitted out with shelving. The area was Holborn and the City of London. It was a turning point in my life. I built up a calling pattern of eighteen shops each day. I didn't eat! I didn't drink! I didn't fornicate! I just worked!

Before the end of '69 I had saved a respectable amount of money and chopped-in my white Mini for a dark blue Ford Capri at Highbury Corner Motors for an amazing deal. The salesman was mesmerized by my banter. I wanted satisfaction for virtually throwing away my Mini-Cooper to buy a MKII 1700 cc Ford Consul in 1966.

I became a loner, driving to Aylesbury virtually every weekend to see Mum. Back at work I did not pick up on the many overtures from female shop manager/assistants. I didn't want to get close.

As with every year, Christmas was upon us — again! Then, New Year. But this time I could remember New Year's Eve into the new decade; just as I had remembered New Year's Eve 10 years earlier with Gina. I decided to go to the Tottenham Royal, on my own. As the time approached for the passover into 1970 I climbed the stairs overlooking the dance floor and leant on the handrail of the balustrading. As I watched the meaningless gyrations/antics and out-of-character behaviour of those beneath me, I determined the maintenance and continuity of my INDIVIDUALITY!